The Passion and Resurrection Narratives of Jesus:
A Commentary

The Passion and Resurrection Narratives of Jesus:
A Commentary

Stephen J. Binz

 THE LITURGICAL PRESS
Collegeville, Minnesota

Cover by Don Bruno.

Nihil obstat: Robert C. Harren, *Censor deputatus.*
Imprimatur: ✠ Jerome Hanus, O.S.B., Bishop of St. Cloud, December 15, 1988.
Scripture quotations are taken from the *New American Bible with Revised New Testament,* copyright © 1986 by the Confraternity of Christian Doctrine, Washington, D.C., and are used by license of copyright owners. All rights reserved.

1	2	3	4	5	6	7	8	9	10

Library of Congress Cataloging-in-Publication Data

Binz, Stephen J., 1955-
    The Passion and Resurrection narratives of Jesus : A commentary/
Stephen J. Binz.
        p.   cm.
    ISBN 0-8146-1771-9
    1. Bible. N.T. Gospels—Commentaries. 2. Passion narratives
(Gospels) 3. Jesus Christ—Resurrection—Biblical teaching.
I. Title.
BS2555.3.B56   1989   88-35692
226'.077—dc19   CIP

Contents

Preface

Though educated in biblical scholarship, I spend my life primarily in pastoral service. It is from this combination of research and ministry that this book has been written. The passion and resurrection is the core of the Scriptures; it is also the heart of faith, liturgy, and prayer. Indebted to the ongoing biblical scholarship of countless others, I have synthesized and reshaped the research for the benefit of a wide audience. I hope the explanations and insights contained in this book will enrich the faith, worship, and prayer of all who look to the crucified and risen Jesus as the source of life.

Although this book represents many solitary hours, it is primarily the result of a community of people. I am grateful to Bishop Andrew McDonald for encouraging my biblical teaching and writing in the midst of pastoral ministry, to my students for their continual challenge, and to my parishioners with whom I am privileged to share Christ's life through the Word and Eucharist. My constant source of enthusiasm and suggestions are the participants and leaders of the Little Rock Scripture Study program, especially Fr. Richard Oswald, Lilly Hess, and Matt Mattingly. I am indebted to Greg Wolfe for his suggestions, and to Fr. Jerome Kodell, O.S.B., for the encouragement to write. I am also grateful to Cackie Upchurch for her generous assistance in typing the manuscript and for her encouragement. Above all, I thank my mother and father, my continual source of faith and life, to whom I dedicate this work.

STEPHEN J. BINZ

Introduction

The very core of the good news of Christianity is the passion, death, and resurrection of Jesus. Paul states the central message of the Church's earliest proclamation: "I handed on to you as of first importance what I also received: that Christ died for our sins in accordance with the scriptures; that he was buried; that he was raised on the third day in accordance with the scriptures; that he appeared to Kephas, then to the Twelve" (1 Cor 15:3-5). All the writings of the New Testament demonstrate that the passion, death, and resurrection was the culmination of Jesus' mission and brought all the words and deeds of his life to a climax.

The passion and resurrection accounts in each of the four Gospels are remarkably similar, considering the vast differences in time and circumstance in which each author wrote. The similarities in the events, sequence, characters, and vocabulary point to the antiquity of the traditions and the deep respect of each writer for the historical remembrances of the original disciples.

Yet when comparing the accounts of the four Gospels what stands out even more clearly are the differences. Too often we hasten to try to reconcile the differences rather than seek to understand what those differences mean. Each writer provides us with a profoundly distinctive contribution to our understanding of Jesus and his saving acts. Writing in a different cultural context with a new set of circumstances for the Christian community, each evangelist presented the early traditions in new ways. Presenting a detailed biography was not the dominant concern of each author; rather, they all interpreted the meaning of Jesus' words and deeds as they listened to the apostolic preaching and followed the guidance of the Holy Spirit. The living word took on new shape according to the needs and circumstances of each community and each generation of Christians.

The early preaching of the Church proclaimed that Jesus' passion, death, and resurrection were "according to the Scriptures." Through the Spirit's guidance the Church came to see how the saving deeds of Jesus brought the saving history of God's people to a culminating fulfillment. They realized, through the prayerful and liturgical reading of the Hebrew Scriptures, how the tragedy and triumph they had experienced in Jesus was in conformity with God's will. In writing their accounts, the evangelists drew on the words of the prophets, the prayers of the psalms, and other texts, to help the Church see God's presence in the paschal events.

Clearly the passion and resurrection accounts are colored by the relationship of the church and the synagogue in each particular generation and locality. The accusations of the Jewish leaders, the portrayal of Pilate, and the reactions of the Jews and the Romans at the final events of Jesus' life vary in each Gospel according to the religious and political climate in which the author lived. Hostile generalizations about the Jewish people, such as "all the people" in Matthew, and "the Jews" in John, reflect later developments in times of competition and persecution. Simplistic accusations about guilt for the death of Jesus, known so well from our painful history, occur when we read the Gospels too literally and fail to critically interpret them.

Each Gospel presents us with a different portrait of Jesus. Just as a scene can be photographed from several different angles to give us a better appreciation of the reality, the person of Jesus can be known and understood more fully because we have four different portraits. All of them are given to us by the inspiring Spirit, yet none of them exhausts the fullness of who Jesus is.

Through a detailed examination of the passion and resurrection accounts of each Gospel, we can experience the person of Jesus more deeply. Through reflection on these accounts, we can understand more fully the central events of our Christian faith. Through seeing how each writer responded to the mystery of Jesus in his own life, we can enter more completely into the saving death and resurrection of Jesus for ourselves.

The Gospel accounts are not just memories from the past; they are a living reality for the present. Like the early Christians, we can identify aspects of our lives with the fearful disciples, the hostile opponents, the vacillating crowds, the betrayer, and the one who denied Jesus. Yet above all, through reading the Gospels we seek to conform our lives to the life of Jesus. He was not just a victim of circumstances, but his suffering and death was the inevitable result of his commitments. By conforming our lives to his passion, not only are we better able to endure our own suffering, but we actively take up the cross, the necessary result of a life committed to others. Likewise, in the resurrection, not only are we assured of eternal life, but we are empowered to live the only kind of life worth living forever.

The Passion and Resurrection According to Mark

We begin our study of the passion and resurrection narratives with the Gospel of Mark. Though the narratives were formed from the earlier traditions of the Christian community, the accounts written by Mark are the earliest extant narratives of Jesus' passion and resurrection. Mark's accounts are also of primary importance because they are the principal source for the Gospels of Matthew and Luke, and possibly even for John.

Though the passion and resurrection form the climactic final chapters of Mark's Gospel, the cross is embedded in Jesus' entire life. Mark, throughout his Gospel, shows how Jesus takes up his cross by choosing a way of life that inevitably leads to rejection, suffering, and death. Jesus' ministry provokes controversy both in Galilee and in Jerusalem. These conflicts with the religious authorities lead to their plotting against Jesus to put him to death (3:6; 11:18). The passion of John the Baptist anticipates the passion of Jesus as it shows that the destiny of a prophet is suffering and rejection.

The question of Jesus, "Who do you say that I am?" (8:29), creates the centrifugal force of the entire Gospel. The question implies that the Gospel is about the identity of Jesus and the struggle of the disciples to understand that identity. The reader is told from the beginning that Jesus is the Messiah and Son of God (1:1), and the disciples will continually struggle to understand this identity of Jesus. In his three predictions of suffering, death, and resurrection (8:31; 9:31; 10:33-34), Jesus reveals that his identity is made known through his destiny. By using the title Son of Man, Jesus shows that he cannot be understood as triumphant except through his suffering and death.

Jesus is most fully revealed on the cross. He who is utterly abandoned by all his disciples and seemingly even by God, is truly the Son of God. Jesus' death becomes the moment of revelation, when the hidden identity of Jesus is made fully known. Through the paradox of the cross the true disciple is able to understand the full meaning of Jesus' messiahship.

The cross not only reveals Jesus' full identity, but it is also the test of true discipleship. "For whoever loses his life for my sake and that of the gospel will save it" (8:35). A disciple is one who willingly gives his life for others as Jesus did. The disciples, too, will be plotted against, betrayed, denied, mocked, abandoned, and persecuted as they anticipate the glorious return of Jesus. The suffering, death, and triumph of Jesus is also the passion of the community of his disciples.

Mark's Gospel is not a tragedy. The Kingdom of God is already present in Jesus and in his community, yet it is hidden in lowliness, suffering, and persecution, just as the glorious identity of Jesus is hidden in his passion. The Gospel anticipates the future as Jesus is confident the Father will raise him from death. Abandoned by his followers, Jesus knows that he will go again to Galilee to gather his scattered flock. There he will lead them in the way of discipleship as they anticipate his return in glory.

Mark 14:1-2

The Conspiracy against Jesus. [1]The Passover and the Feast of Unleavened Bread were to take place in two days' time. So the chief priests and the scribes were seeking a way to arrest him by treachery and put him to death. [2]They said, "Not during the festival, for fear that there may be a riot among the people."

Mark begins his passion account by placing these final events within the context of the Jewish Passover celebration. Each year Passover commemorated the redemption of the Israelites from slavery to freedom. It began, as all Jewish feasts, at sundown. In the afternoon before the feast, the Passover lamb was sacrificed in the Temple. With the Passover supper that evening, the events of the Exodus were retold and remembered. Only unleavened bread was eaten for the supper and for seven days thereafter, remembering the hasty departure from Egypt and the affliction in the desert. Since the Passover was to be celebrated from sundown on Thursday to sundown on Friday, Mark's chronology would place the beginning of the plot against Jesus on Wednesday.

14

Mark identifies the chief priests and the scribes several times during his Gospel. The scribes were the lawyers and theologians of the time. Jesus' conflict with them builds from the beginning of the Gospel (1:22) and comes to a climax at the passion. The chief priests served as advisors to the high priests of Jerusalem. Jesus begins to mention them in his predictions of the passion (8:31). Throughout the second half of the Gospel Jesus continually foretells that the religious leaders will hand him over for death. The religious leaders decided not to arrest Jesus during the feast because they feared his impact on the crowds. Yet, they are not in control and Jesus will die on the very day of Israel's feast of liberation.

Mark 14:3-9

The Anointing at Bethany. ³When he was in Bethany reclining at table in the house of Simon the leper, a woman came with an alabaster jar of perfumed oil, costly genuine spikenard. She broke the alabaster jar and poured it on his head. ⁴There were some who were indignant. "Why has there been this waste of perfumed oil? ⁵It could have been sold for more than three hundred days' wages and the money given to the poor." They were infuriated with her. ⁶Jesus said, "Let her alone. Why do you make trouble for her? She has done a good thing for me. ⁷The poor you will always have with you, and whenever you wish you can do good to them, but you will not always have me. ⁸She has done what she could. She has anticipated anointing my body for burial. ⁹Amen, I say to you, wherever the gospel is proclaimed to the whole world, what she has done will be told in memory of her."

Bethany, where Jesus was lodging during his stay in Jerusalem, was a small village over the brow of the Mount of Olives. No information is given about Simon the leper, but Mark shows how Jesus continued to dine with the outcasts of society. Attention here is on the nameless woman. The story of how she anointed Jesus is a striking contrast to the plotting and treachery of the scenes which precede and follow it.

The flask of oil was a rare and expensive ointment. The woman's pouring it over the head of Jesus is clearly a reference to the Old Testament anointing of kings. Jesus' anointing is a sign of his kingly messiahship, which is emphasized throughout his stay in Jerusalem (11:1-10). This extravagant gesture was challenged by some of the bystanders who argued that those three hundred denarii could have been given to the poor. Giving alms was an important obligation, especially during Passover.

The response of Jesus is sometimes misinterpreted as showing the inevitability of poverty. His response echoes Deuteronomy 15:11, which is actually a command to give to the poor and needy. Jesus reminds them that after his departure, the poor will remain to be cared for. The emphasis here is clearly that they will not always have Jesus because of his imminent death. Jesus interprets the true significance of the scene, a prophetic sign that points toward his death.

The woman is able to understand his approaching death and respond in a lavishly generous way. What she has done will be told in memory of her because in the midst of betrayal the woman showed the response of a true disciple. She and many other women in the Gospel (12:42-44; 15:40-41) respond far more authentically than the inner circle of Jesus' disciples.

Mark ties this story into his passion narrative. It is a symbolic reminder of Jesus' dying and rising. It is an anointing for burial, since the rapidly approaching Sabbath would leave no time for the customary anointing after his death. The story also hints at the resurrection which will make the later anointing by the women at the tomb impossible.

Verse 9 refers to the universal message of the Gospel which Jesus has instructed the community to proclaim "to all the nations" (13:10). This story will be told because it is the good news of Jesus' saving death and the call to respond to it with generous service.

Mark 14:10-11

The Betrayal by Judas. ¹⁰Then Judas Iscariot, one of the Twelve, went off to the chief priests to hand him over to them. ¹¹When they heard him they were pleased and promised to pay him money. Then he looked for an opportunity to hand him over.

Mark connects this scene with the rest of the Gospel by stating that Judas Iscariot was one of the Twelve. Jesus had chosen Judas, as one of the Twelve, to be with him and had given him a share in his teaching and his mission. This scene forms a sharp contrast to the memorable scene of true discipleship which precedes it. The woman generously responds with costly oil, while Judas betrays Jesus for money. Mark uses the scene to contrast true discipleship with failure of discipleship for all future disciples of Jesus.

The words "hand over" are used through Mark's Gospel: from the handing over of John the Baptist (1:14) to the handing over of Jesus, to the future handing over of his disciples (13:9). Those who precede Jesus as his prophets and those who follow him as his disciples are handed over while pursuing their mission.

Mark gives no motivation for Judas' betrayal. The evangelist emphasizes Judas' freedom in making his tragic choice, even though he is part of the cosmic drama of Jesus' death. As he looked for his opportunity, the final plot picks up momentum.

Mark 14:12-16

Preparations for the Passover. ¹²On the first day of the Feast of Unleavened Bread, when they sacrificed the Passover lamb, his disciples said to him, "Where do you want us to go and prepare for you to eat the Passover?" ¹³He sent two of his disciples and said to them, "Go into the city and a man will meet you, carrying a jar of water. Follow him. ¹⁴Wherever he enters, say to the master of the house, 'The Teacher says, "Where is my guest room where I may eat the Passover with my disciples?" ' ¹⁵Then he will show you a large upper room furnished and ready. Make the preparations for us there." ¹⁶The disciples then went off, entered the city, and found it just as he had told them; and they prepared the Passover.

Mark clearly stresses that the meal they were preparing was a Passover supper. He continually reminds the reader of the significance of Israel's central feast of hope and liberation in the context of Jesus' passion. It is now Thursday, the day before Passover, the day for the slaughtering of the Passover lamb. The festival would begin in the evening so all the preparations needed to be made beforehand.

Jesus gives detailed instructions to two of his disciples to go and prepare the room for the Passover meal. They find the man carrying a water jar, an unusual sight since usually only women carried water in such jars, and they find everything just as Jesus had foretold.

This unusually detailed directive is similar to the preparation for Jesus' triumphal entry into Jerusalem (11:1-7). There two disciples were instructed to go to the nearby village where they would find a colt on which no one had ever sat. The two scenes are contrasted by their mood: the first of triumphal entry; the second of the imminent tragedy. Both scenes show the prophetic knowledge of Jesus and his deliberate way of entering into his passion.

Mark 14:17-21

The Betrayer. [17]When it was evening, he came with the Twelve. [18]And as they reclined at table and were eating, Jesus said, "Amen, I say to you, one of you will betray me, one who is eating with me." [19]They began to be distressed and to say to him, one by one, "Surely it is not I?" [20]He said to them, "One of the Twelve, the one who dips with me into the dish. [21]For the Son of Man indeed goes, as it is written of him, but woe to that man by whom the Son of Man is betrayed. It would be better for that man if he had never been born."

The Passover meal is surrounded before and after by Jesus' prediction of betrayal and denial. Mark does not name the betrayer in this scene; he refers to all the disciples who will be shaken in faith and scattered. Mark lets his readers know that they could be the subjects of the same kind of betrayal, scattering, and denial against Jesus.

The scene emphasizes that the betrayer is an intimate companion of Jesus. Notice the progression: "one of you," "one who is eating with me," "one of the Twelve," "one who dips with me into the dish." The betrayal is made even more grievous as the friendship is increasingly affirmed.

The reader is drawn into the shocked response. One by one they ask Jesus, "Surely it is not I?" The reader is called to repeat the question in turn. It is a failure of which every disciple is capable.

In the Psalms of lament the righteous sufferer is betrayed by his friends. Psalm 41:10, "Even my friend who had my trust and partook of my bread, has raised his heel against me," seems to be particularly echoed here (see also Ps 55:13-15).

Again Mark stresses the betrayer's freedom to choose his action. He reminds us that even though the passion of Jesus unfolds in accord with the Scriptures, the betrayer holds full responsibility. The prophetic woe points up the wickedness of the betrayal.

Mark 14:22-26

The Lord's Supper. ²²While they were eating, he took bread, said the blessing, broke it, and gave it to them, and said, "Take it; this is my body." ²³Then he took a cup, gave thanks, and gave it to them, and they all drank from it. ²⁴He said to them, "This is my blood of the covenant, which will be shed for many. ²⁵Amen, I say to you, I shall not drink again the fruit of the vine until the day when I drink it new in the kingdom of God." ²⁶Then, after singing a hymn, they went out to the Mount of Olives.

The actions of Jesus with the bread, as he takes, blesses, breaks, and gives it to his disciples, are the same gestures he performed at the feeding of the five thousand and the four thousand (6:41; 8:6). In the two feeding accounts the bread becomes a profound symbol for his messianic mission as he feeds both Jews and Gentiles. In the disciples' failure to understand the meaning of the loaves (6:52; 8:17-21), Mark shows their failure to understand the person of Jesus and the meaning of his mission.

At the Eucharistic meal, Jesus goes further and identifies the loaf with his body, his very self. As Jesus is about to be handed over, broken, and put to death, this ritual action expresses Jesus' gift of himself for others. As Jesus broke the bread for the crowds, expressing his mission as the Messiah, so his action at the meal expresses the final act of that mission as he gives his very self.

The cup refers to the death of Jesus in other passages of the Gospel (10:38-45; 14:36). In each passage, the disciples are invited to share in his sacrificial death. "To drink the cup God had mixed" was a Jewish expression for the martyrdom a prophet had to undergo. As the disciples drink from it they are joining themselves to a sharing in his death.

Jesus identifies the cup of wine with his blood, the blood of the covenant. Here he evokes the covenant ratified by Moses (Exod 24:8) as he sprinkled the blood of the sacrifice over the altar and on the people. Jesus is saying that his blood, which will be shed at his death, will establish a renewed covenant relationship. "For many" is a semitic expression that is not limited, but indicates the inclusive scope of his mission (10:45).

With another prophetic "amen" phrase, Jesus gives both finality and hope to the scene. No longer will he celebrate the Passover with his disciples. Yet Jesus looks beyond death to the banquet of God's Kingdom. The wine of the banquet is an Old Testament symbol for the abundance of the Kingdom (Isa 25:6-9). The cup of Jesus' death will be transformed into the wine of the coming kingdom. Thus, the celebration of the Eucharist is a remembrance of the saving death of Jesus, and also an anticipation of the kingdom.

The thanksgiving hymn they sang, consisting of Psalms 114–118, concluded the Passover meal. These songs celebrate God's liberating power in bringing the people to freedom. As they go out to the Mount of Olives, across the valley from Jerusalem, Jesus is preparing to fulfill the Passover for all his followers.

Mark 14:27-31

> **Peter's Denial Foretold.** [27]Then Jesus said to them, "All of you will have your faith shaken, for it is written:
>
> 'I will strike the shepherd,
> and the sheep will be dispersed.'
>
> [28]But after I have been raised up, I shall go before you to Galilee." [29]Peter said to him, "Even though all should have their faith shaken, mine will not be." [30]Then Jesus said to him, "Amen, I say to you, this very night before the cock crows twice you will deny me three times." [31]But he vehemently replied, "Even though I should have to die with you, I will not deny you." And they all spoke similarly.

The Last Supper is immediately followed by Jesus' foretelling of desertion and denial by his disciples. Again, as Jesus addresses "all of you," Mark intends to include his readers in this prediction of broken discipleship.

Jesus first tells his disciples that they will all stumble and have their faith shaken. The Greek here literally means "be scandalized." Mark has used this verb before to mean encountering an obstacle that blocks one's faith. In the parable of the sower, the seed which falls on rocky ground is like those who at first receive the word with joy. But when tribulation or persecution comes, they quickly are scandalized. The faith of the disciples is not deep enough to be ready for the tribulation of suffering and death.

Jesus explains their falling away by quoting from Zechariah 13:7. Sheep and shepherd were commonly used metaphors for God and Israel. The Messiah was to be a true shepherd whom God would set over the sheep (Ezek 34:23). Mark had already applied the image to Jesus in the first account of the loaves (Mark 6:34). Now the shepherd would be struck down, and the disciples would be dispersed in disillusionment and fear. Indeed, none of the chosen disciples would remain with him until his death.

As in his prediction of his passion, Jesus follows with a prediction of resurrection and hope. The messenger repeats this promise at the empty tomb of Jesus (16:7). The promised return to Galilee will end Mark's Gospel and fulfill Jesus' promise.

Galilee is the center of Jesus' ministry; Jerusalem is the scene of his passion and death. By going ahead of his disciples to the beginnings of his own ministry, he allows them to once more share in his ministry. This time they will walk the way of discipleship, understanding that it leads to Jerusalem, to death and resurrection.

Peter responds that even if all the others should be scandalized, he will not. Peter's overconfident answer leads Jesus to introduce his third prophecy with the solemn "Amen." Again Peter's inability to accept and understand the necessity of suffering leads to his failure (8:32-34).

Once more Peter rebukes Jesus with a vehement protest (8:32). The other disciples join in the rebuttal. The shallow loyalty of the disciples, as they fail to accept Jesus' words about the cross, forms an ironic conclusion to the dark scene.

Mark 14:32-42

The Agony in the Garden. ³²Then they came to a place named Gethsemane, and he said to his disciples, "Sit here while I pray." ³³He took with him Peter, James, and John, and began to be troubled and distressed. ³⁴Then he said to them, "My soul is sorrowful even to death. Remain here and keep watch." ³⁵He advanced a little and fell to the ground and prayed that if it were possible the hour might pass by him; ³⁶he said, "Abba, Father, all things are possible to you. Take this cup away from me, but not what I will but what you will." ³⁷When he returned he found them asleep. He said to Peter, "Simon are you asleep? Could you not keep watch for one hour? ³⁸Watch and pray that you may not undergo the test. The spirit is willing but the flesh is weak." ³⁹Withdrawing again, he prayed, saying the same thing. ⁴⁰Then he returned once more and found them asleep, for they could not keep their eyes open and did not know what to answer him. ⁴¹He returned a third time and said to them, "Are you still sleeping and taking your rest? It is enough. The hour has come. Behold, the Son of Man is to be handed over to sinners. [42]Get up, let us go. See, my betrayer is at hand."

Gethsemane means "olive press," and is a secluded grove on the slope of the Mount of Olives. Here we witness the anguished prayer of Jesus before he is handed over, and the repeated failure of his closest disciples to watch with him.

Jesus takes with him Peter, James, and John as his intimate companions. It is these three who are present at the Transfiguration (9:2-13) which this scene dramatically contrasts. In both scenes Jesus takes the three disciples aside from the others to reveal the depth of his mission. Just as they witnessed Jesus in glory, they now see him in anguish and weakness as he faces death. If they are to understand Jesus, they must understand his suffering as well as his glory.

These three, along with Andrew, were also the ones who heard his apocalyptic discourse on this same Mount of Olives (13:3-37). There Jesus told the disciples to watch and pray because no one, not even the Son, knows the day or the hour when the events described will take place. Here Jesus relates his own suffering to the tribulation of his disciples throughout time. The attitude of the true disciple must always be watchfulness and expectation.

The words of Jesus' prayer echo the anguished Psalms of Lament. The desolation of abandonment, the terrors of approaching death, the betrayal of friends, yet trust in God's faithfulness—these are the laments of ancient Israel that form on the lips of Jesus as his death approaches.

Jesus addresses his prayer to his Father. The Aramaic word "Abba" is preserved here, because this is the habitual prayer form of Jesus. It expresses the affectionate and reverential address by a Jewish child or adult to a parent. At his baptism and at the transfiguration, Jesus is proclaimed as God's beloved Son. Now the deep union between the Father and the Son is acclaimed by Jesus as he prays in the garden.

As the transfiguration had shown Jesus in his divine glory, the garden scene shows his profound humanity. Overwhelmed by fear and sadness, he prays that the cup be taken away. The prayer is shockingly honest. Throughout the Gospel, Mark has shown Jesus as destined to lay down his life, to "drink the cup." Yet, now as the time approaches, Jesus pours out his heart in a profound and emotional lament.

Still, the bedrock of Jesus' prayer is the Father's will. It is dedication to God's will which guides Mark's presentation of the life of Jesus.

The Son of Man would drink the cup because Jesus understood God's will through his dedicated prayer.

The ardent prayer of Jesus is strongly contrasted with the disciples' behavior. Three times Jesus returns from prayer to find them asleep. Their continual incomprehension and failure to accept the prediction of Jesus' suffering throughout the Gospel prepares us for their failures during the passion. Jesus had predicted their desertion, and now their inability to stay awake with Jesus forecasts the collapse of their discipleship.

Before entering into prayer, Jesus had warned the disciples to "keep watch." These words recall the final words of his apocalyptic discourse: "What I say to you, I say to all: 'Watch!' " Clearly he relates the drowsiness of his three closest disciples to the neglectful tendencies within all his followers. Watchful alertness was to be the posture of discipleship if they were to continue the mission of Jesus in the midst of opposition and persecution.

After each prayer of Jesus the results are the same: the disciples fall asleep instead of keeping watch. Jesus urges them to "watch and pray" that they may not "undergo the test." This is the same verb used to describe the testing of Jesus in the desert at the beginning of the Gospel (1:12-13). This testing, which served as a preface to Jesus' ministry, would continue in the lives of his followers as they struggled with the power of evil in the world. Jesus recognizes the polar dimensions within humanity: the spirit and the flesh. The spirit is responsive to God's will, while the flesh is egotistical and opposed to God's will.

The triple failure of the disciples is contrasted with the threefold prayer of Jesus. After finding them sleeping for a third time, Jesus announces that the hour has come and he is about to be handed over. Through his prayer Jesus is now prepared for the betrayal and passion. However, the disciples who failed to watch in vigilant prayer will flee in fear.

Mark 14:43-52

The Betrayal and Arrest of Jesus. ⁴³Then, while he was still speaking, Judas, one of the Twelve, arrived, accompanied by a crowd with swords and clubs who had come from the chief priests, the scribes, and the elders. ⁴⁴His betrayer had arranged a signal with them, saying, "The man I shall kiss is the one; arrest him and lead

23

him away securely." ⁴⁵He came and immediately went over to him
and said, "Rabbi." And he kissed him. ⁴⁶At this they laid hands
on him and arrested him. ⁴⁷One of the bystanders drew his sword,
struck the high priest's servant, and cut off his ear. ⁴⁸Jesus said
to them in reply, "Have you come out as against a robber, with
swords and clubs, to seize me? ⁴⁹Day after day I was with you
teaching in the temple area, yet you did not arrest me; but that
the scriptures may be fulfilled." ⁵⁰And they all left him and fled.
⁵¹Now a young man followed him wearing nothing but a linen cloth
about his body. They seized him, ⁵²but he left the cloth behind
and ran off naked.

While Jesus was still speaking in the garden, Judas arrived with the
arresting party. The crowd, who had come from the chief priests,
scribes, and elders, represents the Jewish Sanhedrin. It is these religious
leaders of Jerusalem who had been seeking Jesus since their confrontation with him in the temple (11:27).

Judas addressed Jesus as "Rabbi," the honored title by which disciples addressed their master. The kiss further emphasizes that this is
a betrayal of friendship. Jesus is the righteous sufferer who is handed
over by his trusted companion.

The passion predictions that mark the second half of the Gospel
(8:31; 9:31; 10:33) point to this handing over, the arrest of Jesus by
the chief priests, elders, and scribes. The scene is marked by confusion. A bystander draws his sword and strikes the high priest's servant.
No motive is given for the action in Mark's Gospel, though it seems
to be a historical detail that is a result of the mob scene. They came
with swords and clubs to arrest Jesus as if he were a common criminal,
though he had taught openly in the temple. Jesus does not resist arrest
and his final words in this scene set the coming events within the context of God's plan: "that the scriptures may be fulfilled." The reference
here is not to any specific scriptural text, but to the whole of God's
salvific plan, shown through many Old Testament passages that influence the passion scenes.

Jesus' prediction that the shepherd would be struck and the sheep
would be dispersed is here fulfilled (14:27). The complete desertion of
Jesus by his followers is starkly described: "They all left and fled."

A final conclusion to the scene is included only in Mark's Gospel.
A young man who was following Jesus left even his clothing to flee
from the scene. This anonymous follower of Jesus stresses the total

desertion of Jesus by his followers, and challenges the readers of the Gospel to consider their own commitment to remain with Jesus in crisis.

Mark 14:53-65

Jesus before the Sanhedrin. ⁵³They led Jesus away to the high priest, and all the chief priests and the elders and the scribes came together. ⁵⁴Peter followed him at a distance into the high priest's courtyard and was seated with the guards, warming himself at the fire. ⁵⁵The chief priests and the entire Sanhedrin kept trying to obtain testimony against Jesus in order to put him to death, but they found none. ⁵⁶Many gave false witness against him, but their testimony did not agree. ⁵⁷Some took the stand and testified falsely against him, alleging, ⁵⁸"We heard him say, 'I will destroy this temple made with hands and within three days I will build another not made with hands.'" ⁵⁹Even so their testimony did not agree. ⁶⁰The high priest rose before the assembly and questioned Jesus, saying, "Have you no answer? What are these men testifying against you?" ⁶¹But he was silent and answered nothing. Again the high priest asked him and said to him, "Are you the Messiah, the son of the Blessed One?" ⁶²Then Jesus answered, "I am;

and 'you will see the Son of Man
seated at the right hand of the Power
and coming with the clouds of heaven.'"

⁶³At that the high priest tore his garments and said, "What further need have we of witnesses? ⁶⁴You have heard the blasphemy. What do you think?" They all condemned him as deserving to die. ⁶⁵Some began to spit on him. They blindfolded him and struck him and said to him, "Prophesy!" And the guards greeted him with blows.

The scene now shifts to the court of the high priest. Mark sets the scene as a formal trial before the Sanhedrin. This council, made up of seventy representatives from the chief priests, elders, and scribes, governed the Jews in those religious and political affairs allowed to them by the occupying Romans. The Sanhedrin was led by the high priest, Caiaphas, though he is not named by Mark.

Peter is present outside the trial. Though all the followers of Jesus had fled in Gethsemane, Peter's presence recalls his words at the Last Supper: "Even though all should have their faith shaken, mine will not be." Yet, despite Peter's insistence, Jesus predicts his denial. The result of his conviction is hinted at here as he follows Jesus, but "at a distance."

25

The witnesses at the trial focus on Jesus' relationship to the temple. Jesus had already critiqued the temple worship (11:17) and predicted its destruction (13:2). In the apocalyptic discourse of chapter 13, Mark has symbolically related the destruction of the temple and the death of the messiah. In the trial, the witnesses cast Jesus as the one who will destroy the present temple and build another not made with hands.

Mark clearly associates each of Jesus' references to the temple with the plot on Jesus' life (11:18; 12:12; 14:1). If the accusation against Jesus was indeed his intention to destroy the temple, his arrest and trial would be a natural consequence. The witnesses fail to agree, however, and Jesus neither admits nor denies their accusation.

Mark allows the accusation to remain ambiguous. On one level the statement is clearly a false witness to the ministry of Jesus. Jesus is not a militant who intended to destroy the temple building but rather the Messiah who will himself be destroyed. Yet on another level, the messianic ministry and death of Jesus destroyed the need and efficacy of the temple and established the new, spiritual temple of the Christian community.

While the destruction of the temple may have been interpreted as a revolutionary claim, the promise to rebuild the temple is a messianic declaration. In Jewish literature at the time of Jesus there was an expectation that the Messiah would establish a new and transformed temple for authentic worship. The destruction and renewal of the temple is related to the death and resurrection of Jesus. The new order of true worship will be established by Jesus' destruction and triumph.

The climax of the trial comes when the high priest asks Jesus: "Are you the Messiah, the son of the Blessed One?" The response of Jesus is immediate: "I am." The question brings together the two central titles of Jesus' identity for Mark's Gospel: Christ and Son of God.

Mark first states these two titles in the opening of the Gospel as he identifies Jesus and sets the purpose of his writing. The first half of Mark's Gospel leads to the climactic profession of Peter's faith: "You are the Messiah" (8:29). The title, Son of God, previously proclaimed at Jesus' baptism (1:11) and transfiguration (9:7), will be dramatically revealed by the centurion at the cross (15:39). His identity, which remains hidden and misunderstood by his followers throughout the Gospel, now comes to be fully revealed in his passion. It is only in the context of the cross that Jesus can be fully understood and only now does he accept his messianic titles unreservedly.

It is the title, Son of Man, which adds the dimension of the cross to Jesus' messiahship. Jesus used it throughout the second half of the Gospel to complete the more exalted titles; he used the Son of Man designation every time he referred to his death (8:31; 9:9, 12, 31; 10:33, 45; 14:21, 41). Here at the trial, Jesus uses the Son of Man title as a prediction of triumph. It refers to Jesus' exaltation at the right hand of God and to his victorious power. Two texts are referred to here showing Jesus' triumph: Daniel 7:13, which speaks of a triumphant figure in human form coming with the clouds of heaven, and Psalm 110:1 in which the king is addressed by God, "Sit at my right hand." The triumphant power of Jesus can only be understood and revealed in the context of his giving his life through the cross.

The high priest dramatically tears his garments and labels the prophecy as blasphemy. The tearing of the garments as a response to blasphemy is attested by King Hezekiah in 2 Kings 19:1. The Sanhedrin unanimously and unhesitatingly condemned Jesus as deserving to die. The scene ends as they mock Jesus as a false prophet, while ironically one of his prophecies, the denial of Peter, is being fulfilled in the courtyard below.

Mark 14:66-72

Peter's Denial of Jesus. ⁶⁶While Peter was below in the courtyard, one of the high priest's maids came along. ⁶⁷Seeing Peter warming himself, she looked intently at him and said, "You too were with the Nazarene, Jesus." ⁶⁸But he denied it saying, "I neither know nor understand what you are talking about." So he went out into the outer court. [Then the cock crowed.] ⁶⁹The maid saw him and began again to say to the bystanders, "This man is one of them." ⁷⁰Once again he denied it. A little later the bystanders said to Peter once more, "Surely you are one of them; for you too are a Galilean." ⁷¹He began to curse and to swear, "I do not know this man about whom you are talking." ²⁷And immediately a cock crowed a second time. Then Peter remembered the word that Jesus had said to him, "Before the cock crows twice you will deny me three times." He broke down and wept.

Mark creates a strange contrast by framing the scene of Peter in the courtyard around the scene of Jesus before the Sanhedrin. As Jesus boldly confesses his messiahship, Peter cowardly denies him.

The accusations against Peter spread from a private question by the maid to a confrontation with all the bystanders. Likewise, Peter's

denials begin as an evasive misunderstanding but develop into a fright-
ened cursing and a sworn rejection of his relationship with Jesus.

Peter's denial fulfills Jesus' prophecy (14:30). The second cockcrow
was the dreadful reminder that caused Peter to weep with remorse. Now
Jesus, abandoned by the last disciple, faces his passion alone.

Mark does not try to hide the embarrassing story of Peter. Writing
in a community that was undergoing persecution, the failure of Peter
became both a warning against unfaithful discipleship and a message
of hope for those who had failed and needed reconciliation.

Mark 15:1-5

Jesus before Pilate. ¹As soon as morning came, the chief priests
with the elders and the scribes, that is, the whole Sanhedrin, held
a council. They bound Jesus, led him away, and handed him over
to Pilate. ²Pilate questioned him, "Are you the king of the Jews?"
He said to him in reply, "You say so." ³The chief priests accused
him of many things. ⁴Again Pilate questioned him, "Have you no
answer? See how many things they accuse you of." ⁵Jesus gave
him no further answer, so that Pilate was amazed.

A major segment of the passion account begins as Jesus is handed
over to the Romans. The third passion prediction (10:33-34) becomes
the prologue for the passion events: "They will condemn him to death
and hand him over to the Gentiles . . ." The trial before the Roman
governor turns from a religious to a political hearing. Though the Jewish officials hand Jesus over, it will be the Roman authorities who will
put him to death.

The role of Pilate must have been well known to Mark's readers
since he is mentioned without introduction. He was the Roman procurator of Judea from 26–35 A.D. His questioning of Jesus parallels that
of the high priest, except Pilate stresses the political side of the issues.

He immediately asks Jesus if he is the King of the Jews. This parallels
the religious question "Are you the Messiah, the son of the Blessed
One?" (14:61). Instead of the affirmative response given to the Sanhedrin, Jesus answers ambiguously. He does not fully claim the title because of its exalted, political connotations. Yet, Jesus does not deny
it because his kingship is a fundamental truth of his identity.

Jesus gives no further response to their accusations. As the righteous suffering servant (Isa 53:7), he will remain silent until the final

lament at his death. Jesus becomes the model for those who suffer unjustly. He had warned his followers at his final discourse that they would be handed over to the courts and arraigned before governors and kings (13:9). Later disciples of Jesus must be prepared to endure the same for the gospel.

Mark 15:6-15

The Sentence of Death. ⁶Now on the occasion of the feast he used to release to them one prisoner whom they requested. ⁷A man called Barabbas was then in prison along with the rebels who had committed murder in a rebellion. ⁸The crowd came forward and began to ask him to do for them as he was accustomed. ⁹Pilate answered, "Do you want me to release to you the king of the Jews?" ¹⁰For he knew that it was out of envy that the chief priests had handed him over. ¹¹But the chief priests stirred up the crowd to have him release Barabbas for them instead. ¹²Pilate again said to them in reply, "Then what [do you want] me to do with [the man you call] the king of the Jews?" ¹³They shouted again, "Crucify him." ¹⁴Pilate said to them, "Why? What evil has he done?" They only shouted the louder, "Crucify him." ¹⁵So Pilate, wishing to satisfy the crowd, released Barabbas to them and, after he had Jesus scourged, handed him over to be crucified.

The custom of releasing a prisoner at Passover seems to have been a concession to the Jews on the part of the Roman government. The name Barabbas literally means "son of the father," providing an ironic choice between him and the true Son of the Father. The choice rests with the crowd, though they are prompted by the chief priests to call for Barabbas.

Pilate is reluctant to condemn Jesus and seems not to believe the charge, but he is pressured by the crowd. Crucifixion is a Roman penalty used against criminals, runaway slaves, and political insurgents. If the Jews had put Jesus to death it would have been by stoning since that was the punishment for blasphemy (Lev 24:16).

Once again Mark uses the term "handed over" to describe the final transfer of Jesus. Judas had handed Jesus over to the chief priest, the priests had handed him over to Pilate, and now Pilate hands Jesus over to be crucified. The disciple, the Jewish leaders, and the Roman leader all share in the responsibility for Jesus' death.

29

Mark 15:16-20

Mockery by the Soldiers. [16]The soldiers led him away inside the palace, that is, the praetorium, and assembled the whole cohort. [17]They clothed him in purple and, weaving a crown of thorns, placed it on him. [18]They began to salute him with, "Hail, King of the Jews!" [19]and kept striking his head with a reed and spitting upon him. They knelt before him in homage. [20]And when they had mocked him, they stripped him of the purple cloak, dressed him in his own clothes, and led him out to crucify him.

The mockery of Jesus continues the fulfillment of Jesus' passion prediction: "who will mock him, spit upon him, scourge him, and put him to death" (10:34). The mockery of the Roman soldiers parallels the first scene of mocking by the Jewish leaders. The Jewish trial ended with his mocking as a prophet, the Roman trial with his mocking as a king. Again Jesus suffers as the innocent servant of Isaiah as he is beaten and spit upon (Isa 50:6).

The purple cloak is the color of royal garments and the crown of thorns mocks the claim to kingship. The taunts of the soldiers take up the accusation at the trial, "King of the Jews." Irony pervades the scene because what the soldiers say and do is true, but on a level they cannot comprehend. Jesus is worthy of their homage, but the true nature of his kingship is hidden in lowly suffering.

Mark 15:21-32

The Way of the Cross. [21]They pressed into service a passer-by, Simon, a Cyrenian, who was coming in from the country, the father of Alexander and Rufus, to carry his cross.
The Crucifixion. [22]They brought him to the place of Golgotha (which is translated Place of the Skull). [23]They gave him wine drugged with myrrh, but he did not take it. [24]Then they crucified him and divided his garments by casting lots for them to see what each should take. [25]It was nine o'clock in the morning when they crucified him. [26]The inscription of the charge against him read, "The King of the Jews." [27]With him they crucified two revolutionaries, one on his right and one on his left.[28] [29]Those passing by reviled him, shaking their heads and saying, "Aha! You who would destroy the temple and rebuild it in three days, [30]save yourself by coming down from the cross." [31]Likewise the chief priests, with

the scribes, mocked him among themselves and said, "He saved others; he cannot save himself. ³²Let the Messiah, the King of Israel, come down now from the cross that we may see and believe." Those who were crucified with him also kept abusing him.

Simon was probably a diaspora Jew who had come to Jerusalem from Cyrene in northern Africa for Passover. He and his sons, Alexander and Rufus, may have later become Christians since their names are known to the Christian community. The words used here, "carry (take up) his cross," are the same words Jesus used when first teaching his disciples about the way of suffering: "Whoever wishes to come after me must deny himself, take up his cross, and follow me" (8:34). Simon's action is a reminder to Mark's community of the way to discipleship.

Crucifixion took place outside the walls of the city, so Jesus would have been led out the city gate. Mark preserves the Aramaic name, Golgotha, for the place of execution, though he translated it for his audience as "Place of the Skull." The name most likely refers to the shape of the hill and to the executions which were a common occurrence there.

Giving wine drugged with myrrh to Jesus was probably an act of mercy which is attested to in other Jewish writings (Prov 31:6). Although the wine was meant to relieve the pain, Mark notes that Jesus refused it, emphasizing the full extent of his suffering.

The crucifixion of Jesus is stated as a matter of fact with no details given of the method or the physical agony. The emphasis is on the details surrounding the crucifixion: the dividing of his garments and the mockery.

The Christian community looked to the Scriptures as prophecies of Jesus' suffering and as avenues to understand the meaning of his death. Psalm 22 seems to have been particularly important as a foreshadowing of the events surrounding the crucifixion. Several of its verses are quoted or alluded to in this section: the act of crucifixion (v. 17), the casting of lots for his garments (v. 19), and the mockery by the crowds (vs. 8-9).

The charge against Jesus and the mockery again recall the true identity of Jesus and his messianic mission. The inscription of the charge "The King of the Jews," meant as a humiliation, ironically states the truth of Jesus' identity. Here, over the cross, the title can be understood in its fullest sense.

Those crucified with Jesus are traditionally called "thieves." Yet, the Greek term also means "revolutionaries," and it is more probable that they were crucified for political insurrection against the Roman occupation. Symbolically the two, "one on his right and one on his left," become his royal court. When James and John had asked for the places of honor in the kingdom, "one at your right and one at your left," Jesus promised them instead a share in his passion. Mark again reminds his readers that the places of honor in the kingdom belong to those who share in the cross.

The mockery of Jesus is done by three distinct groups. First, those passing by take up the charge of the Sanhedrin trial that Jesus will destroy the temple. They challenge him to save himself by coming down from the cross. This is clearly a reference to Psalm 22:8-9. Second, the Jewish leaders continue the charge from his trial and mock his pretension to be "the Messiah, the King of Israel." "He saved others; he cannot save himself" is ironically true concerning his mission: "Whoever wishes to save his life will lose it, but whoever loses his life for my sake and that of the gospel will save it" (8:35). The challenge to come down from the cross in order that they might believe summarizes the temptation of the entire Gospel: only a messiah without the cross is believable. Third, even those crucified with him mock him from the cross. Jesus is reviled by all levels of society, from the ordinary observers, to the Jewish leaders, to the criminals. He is rejected, abandoned, and left totally alone to face his death.

Mark 15:33-41

The Death of Jesus. ³³At noon darkness came over the whole land until three in the afternoon. ³⁴And at three o'clock Jesus cried out in a loud voice, *"Eloi, Eloi, lema sabachthani?"* which is translated, "My God, my God, why have you forsaken me?" ³⁵Some of the bystanders who heard it said, "Look, he is calling Elijah." ³⁶One of them ran, soaked a sponge with wine, put it on a reed, and gave it to him to drink, saying, "Wait, let us see if Elijah comes to take him down." ³⁷Jesus gave a loud cry and breathed his last. ³⁸The veil of the sanctuary was torn in two from top to bottom. ³⁹When the centurion who stood facing him saw how he breathed his last he said, "Truly this man was the Son of God!" ⁴⁰There were also women looking on from a distance. Among them were Mary Magdalene, Mary the mother of the younger James and of Joses, and Salome. ⁴¹These women had followed him when he was in Galilee

and ministered to him. There were also many other women who
had come up with him to Jerusalem.

Mark's passion account is organized in patterns of threes: Jesus'
prayer in Gethsemane is threefold, Peter denies Jesus three times, three
groups mock him on the cross, and the crucifixion consists of three pe-
riods of three hours each. At the third hour (9 a.m.) Jesus was crucified, at the sixth hour (noon) darkness came over the land, and at the
ninth hour (3 p.m.) Jesus died.

The darkness that came over the land recalls the words of the
prophets: Amos 8:9; Joel 2:10; Isaiah 13:10. This association of Jesus'
death with the apocalyptic Day of the Lord emphasizes its cosmic consequences. It also suggests the darkness that was the result of the ninth
plague of Egypt. As the darkness preceded God's saving event in the
Exodus, so, too, it precedes the saving death of Jesus.

The great cry of Jesus expresses his anguish. He has been forsaken
by all his followers, and now in his final hour he feels the depth of
abandonment in even the absence of God. The cry is the opening verse
of Psalm 22, and we may assume that Jesus continued the psalm as
his final prayer. It expresses the desolation of the suffering one, yet
holds to confident trust. Psalm 22, so often referred to in the passion
account, ends not in despair, but in triumph and deliverance. It
proclaims the eventual worship of God by all the nations.

Even this final prayer of Jesus is mocked by the bystanders and misunderstood as a desperate call to Elijah rather than "my God" (*Eloi*,
in Aramaic). Their confusion is filled with irony since Elijah had already returned through the ministry of John the Baptist. It was his being handed over, his imprisonment and violent death, that prepared
the way for the passion of Jesus. The ridicule continues as a bystander
offers Jesus wine soaked into a sponge. This was intended for reviving
him to mockingly give Elijah time for the rescue.

The death of Jesus is the climax of Mark's Gospel and brings to a
head the theological themes he has been developing. The moment of
death is portrayed with absolute stark brutality. The other Gospel
writers describe Jesus' death by emphasizing his control and resignation. In Mark, the scene is pierced by Jesus' loud scream as he breathes
his last.

As Jesus dies, again the scene flashes back to the temple. The cur-
tain separating the holy place from the holy of holies (Exod 26:31-37)
is torn in two from top to bottom. Entry through the veil into the holy

of holies was forbidden to all except the high priest, and for him only once a year. On the great Day of Atonement, a day of sacrifice, penance, and fasting, the high priest entered behind the veil to offer incense and to sprinkle the blood of a sacrificial bull and goat.

Mark associates the death of Jesus with the destruction of the temple. The tearing of the veil is a portent of the impending destruction that occurred in 70 A.D., about the time of Mark's writing. Through the death of Jesus the redemptive significance of the temple sacrifice has been nullified. The offerings in the temple had been for atonement, and that is the meaning of Jesus' death. He fulfills the function of the temple in a new and decisive way. Through his ultimate sacrifice, the obstacles are removed on the way to God.

The death of Jesus opens the way to God for all humanity, Gentiles as well as Jews. The Gentile centurion speaks the climactic declaration of the Gospel as he declares, "Truly this man was the Son of God." The theology of Mark's Gospel is summarized as Jesus' identity is fully expressed for the first time. It is only on the cross that the messianic identity of Jesus can be fully understood and that his sonship can be proclaimed.

The two motifs of the trial here come to their full expression. The destruction of the temple made with hands is now beginning, and the messianic sonship of Jesus is now able to be recognized by all people. The temple not made with hands, of which Jesus is the cornerstone, will be truly open to all, "a house of prayer for all peoples" (11:17). The new, sacred place of worship is the Christian community, the gathering of all who are able to recognize Jesus as the Son of God.

The faith of the Gentile centurion, together with the faithfulness of the women who continue to follow Jesus to his death, again emphasizes the absence of his chosen disciples. Those who are faithful—the centurion, the women, Joseph of Arimathea—represent what the Christian community will be. Women and men, Gentiles and Jews, together form that community called to share the humble, loving, self-giving life of Jesus.

Mark 15:42-47

The Burial of Jesus. ⁴²When it was already evening, since it was the day of preparation, the day before the sabbath, ⁴³Joseph of Arimathea, a distinguished member of the council, who was himself awaiting the kingdom of God, came and courageously went to Pilate and asked for the body of Jesus. ⁴⁴Pilate was amazed that he was already dead. He summoned the centurion and asked him if Jesus had already died. ⁴⁵And when he learned of it from the centurion, he gave the body to Joseph. ⁴⁶Having bought a linen cloth, he took him down, wrapped him in the linen cloth and laid him in a tomb that had been hewn out of the rock. Then he rolled a stone against the entrance to the tomb. ⁴⁷Mary Magdalene and Mary the mother of Joses watched where he was laid.

Again, Mark makes the transition by taking note of the time. It is now Friday evening, the end of preparation day for the Sabbath. Very little information is given about Joseph of Arimathea, who is spoken of here for the first time. He is an influential man, and his "awaiting the kingdom of God" seems to indicate his responsiveness to Jesus' teaching (1:15). His membership on the council may or may not refer to the Sanhedrin.

The fearlessness of Joseph in requesting the body of Jesus is noted in contrast to the cowardly dispersal of the disciples. Joseph does what the disciples of Jesus should have done. He courageously associates himself with the crucified Jesus and gives him a proper burial.

The burial of Jesus prepares for the account of the empty tomb. The reality of Jesus' death is stressed by the reaction of Pilate and it is confirmed by the centurion. Jesus' body is then wrapped in a linen cloth and placed in a tomb that had been hewn out of rock. Mark notes carefully the great stone which sealed the entrance of the tomb and the women who watched where Jesus was laid.

Mark 16:1-8

The Resurrection of Jesus. ¹When the sabbath was over, Mary Magdalene, Mary, the mother of James, and Salome bought spices so that they might go and anoint him. ²Very early when the sun had risen, on the first day of the week, they came to the tomb. ³They were saying to one another, "Who will roll back the stone for us from the entrance to the tomb?" ⁴When they looked up, they saw that the stone had been rolled back; it was very large. ⁵On entering the tomb they saw a young man sitting on the right side, clothed in a white robe, and they were utterly amazed. ⁶He said to them, "Do not be amazed! You seek Jesus of Nazareth, the crucified. He has been raised; he is not here. Behold the place where

> they laid him. ⁷But go and tell his disciples and Peter, 'He is going
> before you to Galilee; there you will see him, as he told you.'"
> ⁸Then they went out and fled from the tomb, seized with trem-
> bling and bewilderment. They said nothing to anyone, for they
> were afraid.

The three women who looked on from a distance at Jesus' death
(15:40) are the women who brought spices with the intention of anointing the body of Jesus. Once again it is the women who attended to Jesus'
needs, the same women who had ministered to him while in Galilee.
The only name that is consistent in the four Gospel accounts of the
empty tomb is Mary Magdalene. The consistency in recounting that
she was the first to discover the empty tomb rests on historical remembrance. A woman in the Judaism of that day could not serve as a witness in any legal proceedings. Thus, the writer would not have cited
women as the first to witness that the tomb was empty unless it was
based on historical remembrance.

Mark points out that the discovery was made "very early when the
sun had risen, on the first day of the week." All was beginning anew,
as if the week of creation had begun again on the first day. The dawn
brought a fresh beginning to the lives of those who had fled in denial
and desertion.

The huge stone rolled away from the entrance to the tomb becomes
part of the portentous sign of the empty tomb. The young man clothed
in white is the interpreting angel, a common feature of apocalyptic writings. The encounter is formulated in the common pattern of angelic
messages: the angel appears, the receivers are fearful, the angel tells
them not to fear and gives the explanation, a commission is given to
the hearers (Luke 1:11f; 1:26f).

In a clear and concise way, Mark relates to the readers the fact of
the empty tomb and the reason for its emptiness. He offers no details
about the resurrection, but briefly states, "He has been raised." The
commission to "go and tell his disciples and Peter" does not seem to
have been fulfilled. They fled from the tomb and said nothing to anyone because of their fear and bewilderment.

Mark ends his Gospel with verse 8. He refrains from describing any
resurrection appearances, though he certainly knew of them and could
have recounted them in his Gospel. The vocabulary and style of the
longer and shorter endings indicate that they were written at a later
period by someone other than Mark. So our study of Mark's writing

should end here. The other endings were probably added because of the discomfort felt by later Christians in comparing the abrupt ending of Mark's account with the elaborate resurrection appearances in the other Gospels.

Why did Mark end his Gospel here? Remember that Mark was writing to teach people in a later generation how to be disciples of Jesus. Thus, Mark leaves his Gospel open-ended. The women flee from the tomb puzzled over the meaning of the resurrection and its implications for their lives. They say nothing to anyone because it is up to each individual to come to know and experience the risen presence of Jesus. Mark leaves the Gospel incomplete because the good news of Jesus is incomplete. It must be taken up and proclaimed by people in every generation.

The message given to the women repeats the promise Jesus made to Peter and the disciples before his agony in the garden. After predicting the desertion of Peter and the disciples, Jesus assured them, "After I have been raised up, I shall go before you to Galilee" (14:28). The messenger proclaims that they will see him there. The final message of the Gospel is that Jesus has again gone ahead of them. Jesus leads and all who hear the good news are challenged to follow him. Jesus' first call to his disciples in Galilee, "Come after me," becomes the final challenge addressed to all future disciples.

Mark wants to tell his readers that the resurrection is not the end of the story, but only a new beginning. What has begun in Jesus is still going on. Jesus, now risen, continues to lead disciples. They are to continue giving life and hope to those in need, continue giving meaning to suffering and bringing life from death. They are to continue hearing the call of Jesus to follow where he leads.

Mark 16:9-20

THE LONGER ENDING

The Appearance to Mary Magdalene. [⁹When he had risen, early on the first day of the week, he appeared first to Mary Magdalene, out of whom he had driven seven demons. ¹⁰She went and told his companions who were mourning and weeping. ¹¹When they heard that he was alive and had been seen by her, they did not believe.

The Appearance to Two Disciples. ¹²After this he appeared in another form to two of them walking along on their way to the country. [13]They returned and told the others; but they did not believe them either.

The Commissioning of the Eleven. [14][But] later, as the eleven were at table, he appeared to them and rebuked them for their unbelief and hardness of heart because they had not believed those who saw him after he had been raised. [15]He said to them, "Go into the whole world and proclaim the gospel to every creature. [16]Whoever believes and is baptized will be saved; whoever does not believe will be condemned. [17]These signs will accompany those who believe: in my name they will drive out demons, they will speak new languages. [18]They will pick up serpents [with their hands], and if they drink any deadly thing, it will not harm them. They will lay hands on the sick, and they will recover."

The Ascension of Jesus. [19]So then the Lord Jesus, after he spoke to them, was taken up into heaven and took his seat at the right hand of God. [20]But they went forth and preached everywhere, while the Lord worked with them and confirmed the word through accompanying signs.]

Today it is generally agreed that Mark intentionally ended his Gospel with verse 8, but in earlier centuries this was not the belief. The common opinion was that the complete ending of Mark's Gospel had been lost. This was evidently the opinion at the end of the first century when the other endings were written. Christians of later decades added endings that they thought Mark would have added himself.

The longer ending contains vocabulary, themes, and a style unlike anything in Mark's Gospel. It is simply a compilation and reformulation of familiar resurrection scenes from the other three Gospels.

The shorter ending appears after verse 8 in several later manuscripts of the Gospel. It was another attempt by early Christians to end Mark's Gospel more smoothly.

The endings have traditionally been accepted as a canonical part of the Gospel. Yet, for our reflection we should leave Mark's work to stand on its own. Only by ending the Gospel with verse 8 can Mark's complete intention and plan be understood. His Gospel ending is far more inspiring and challenging as he leaves it to his readers to relive and continue the Gospel in their lives.

The Passion and Resurrection According to Matthew

The primary source of Matthew's passion account is the Gospel of Mark. Matthew follows Mark's basic sequence and includes every episode from his account. Yet, while they are strikingly similar, there are very important differences since every addition, deletion, and rearrangement in Matthew is done for a purpose. It is primarily through these differences that we are able to see how Matthew reinterprets Mark and develops his own theological themes.

Matthew heightens the dignity and majestic quality of Jesus throughout his passion account. While retaining Mark's emphasis on Jesus' suffering and abandonment, it is clearly the all-knowing and all-powerful Son of God who suffers. Jesus undergoes his passion with full prophetic knowledge of what will happen and with full control over those events. Yet Jesus does not use his power and authority to save himself, but he remains the faithful Son of the Father. The identity of Jesus is not hidden as in Mark, so the dramatic quality of the unfolding of Jesus' identity is lessened. The drama of Matthew lies in Jesus' rejection by those he came to save.

Matthew wrote in a period of the Church characterized by extreme tension with Judaism. The Church and Synagogue had separated, and Christianity was becoming more Gentile in its character. Matthew demonstrates that Jesus is firmly embedded in the salvation history of Israel and that he fulfills God's messianic promises to the people. He also shows how the death and resurrection of Jesus foretells the conversion of the Gentiles and the opening of salvation to all peoples.

As the leaders of Israel refuse to recognize Jesus and reject the Messiah, Israel loses its exclusive privileges as God's people. Matthew is intent on showing how the Church is composed of both Jews and Gentiles. While not excluding Israel, the Kingdom of God is broadened to include all the nations. The promises made to Israel are carried on through the Church as the death and resurrection inaugurates a new age of salvation.

The Gospel ends not only with the promise as in Mark, but with fulfillment. The appearance of Jesus assures the disciples that he is present with them as they continue the mission he left for them. The proclamation of the Gospel and the gathering of God's people is the task of the Church until the end of the age. The resurrection is a foretaste of the final glorious coming of Jesus. He comes to his disciples with full authority as the triumphant Son of God. He assures his community of disciples that he is with them always as they take up their universal mission.

Matthew 26:1-5

The Conspiracy against Jesus. ¹When Jesus finished all these words, he said to his disciples, ²"You know that in two days' time it will be Passover, and the Son of Man will be handed over to be crucified." ³Then the chief priests and the elders of the people assembled in the palace of the high priest, who was called Caiaphas, ⁴and they consulted together to arrest Jesus by treachery and put him to death. ⁵But they said, "Not during the festival, that there may not be a riot among the people."

Matthew begins his passion account by emphasizing that Jesus is in control of the events that are to happen. Jesus instructs his disciples concerning the impending events of his arrest and crucifixion. This is the fourth and last in a series of passion predictions (16:21; 17:22-23; 20:18-19) which show that the passion is integral to the whole life and mission of Jesus.

The opening phrase, "When Jesus finished all these words," is used by Matthew to mark the major transitions of his Gospel. It concludes each of the five great discourses that form the principal structure of the Gospel (also 7:28; 11:1; 13:53; 19:1). Matthew adds here the word "all" which indicates that Jesus has now finished his ministry of instructing his disciples. The last discourse of Jesus was his apocalyptic discourse (Matt 24–25) concerning the end of the ages. The transition links Jesus' teaching ministry with his passion, and juxtaposes the glorious

Son of Man of the apocalyptic discourse with the suffering Son of Man about to undergo the passion.

Matthew makes the connection between the Passover and the death of Jesus explicit. By placing this juxtaposition in the prediction of Jesus, the evangelist shows the connection is not accidental, but part of God's plan. The death of Jesus and its remembrance in the Last Supper form the true Passover sacrifice of the new people of God.

The second half of this double scene contrasts the knowledge and openness of Jesus with the secrecy and treachery of the plotters. Just as the Jewish leaders had gathered around Herod to plot against Jesus' life during his infancy (2:4), now they conspire with the high priest to put Jesus to death. Matthew is the only synoptic Gospel writer to identify the high priest as Caiaphas. Though the leaders decide not to arrest Jesus during the feast of Passover because the multitude of pilgrims could easily start a riot, the prophetic words of Jesus have made the timing inevitable.

Matthew 26:6-13

The Anointing at Bethany. ⁶Now when Jesus was in Bethany in the house of Simon the leper, ⁷a woman came up to him with an alabaster jar of costly perfumed oil, and poured it on his head while he was reclining at table. ⁸When his disciples saw this, they were indignant and said, "Why this waste? ⁹It could have been sold for much, and the money given to the poor." ¹⁰Since Jesus knew this, he said to them, "Why do you make trouble for the woman? She has done a good thing for me. ¹¹The poor you will always have with you; but you will not always have me. ¹²In pouring this perfumed oil upon my body, she did it to prepare me for burial. ¹³Amen, I say to you, wherever this gospel is proclaimed in the whole world, what she has done will be spoken of, in memory of her."

All four evangelists describe the anointing of Jesus by a woman. Luke does not connect the account with the passion, but rather states that the woman is a sinner and associates the scene with Jesus' forgiveness (Luke 7:36-50). The other Gospels locate the scene at Bethany and link it with the passion of Jesus. Matthew closely follows Mark's account, while abbreviating it and omitting a few concrete details such as identifying the oil as "pure nard" and mentioning the cost of the oil.

Matthew identifies those who became indignant at the action of the woman as "disciples." The devotion and insight of the woman contrasts sharply with that of the disciples and prepares for their desertion. As in Mark, this beautiful scene is inserted in the midst of plotting and betrayal. The woman stands out through her faithfulness and her understanding of Jesus' fate.

Jesus praises the woman's action and interprets it as his anointing for burial. This anointing is particularly important here because, unlike in Mark's account, the women will not go to the tomb with the intention of anointing Jesus' body.

Jesus strongly defends the action of the woman from the reproach of the disciples. Concern for the poor is not at question here since Matthew's Gospel clearly shows the importance of giving to the poor for Jesus' followers (19:21; 25:35). The disciples will be continually challenged to be concerned for the poor, but the urgency of the passion calls for an immediate response because of Jesus' imminent departure.

Jesus announces that this will be remembered wherever the good news is proclaimed. Her act of true discipleship will stand out in Matthew's story of salvation as it is proclaimed throughout the world.

Matthew 26:14-16

> **The Betrayal of Judas.** ¹⁴Then one of the Twelve, who was called Judas Iscariot, went to the chief priests ¹⁵and said, "What are you willing to give me if I hand him over to you?" They paid him thirty pieces of silver, ¹⁶and from that time on he looked for an opportunity to hand him over.

Matthew gives special attention to the role of Judas. He expands the material given to him by Mark whenever Judas appears. He adds a monetary motive for the betrayal, Judas' question at the Last Supper asking if he is the betrayer, and the account of his suicide.

The scenes of anointing and betrayal are closely linked and contrasted. The woman's act of love precedes Judas' act of treachery. As the woman anoints Jesus for burial, Judas begins the process that leads to his death. As Jesus shows his disregard for money, Judas bargains for a price.

Matthew extends the factual reporting of Mark into a dialogue between Judas and the chief priests. He shows us that one of the motives for betrayal is money. The heinous nature of the crime is emphasized by Judas' bargaining.

Matthew's Gospel continually stresses the corrupting influence of money. Jesus had previously stated: "No one can serve two masters. He will either hate one and love the other, or be devoted to one and despise the other. You cannot serve God and mammon" (6:24). In his instruction to his disciples, Jesus prohibits them from carrying silver on their mission (10:9; see also 6:19-21; 19:23). Judas' desire for money leads him to abandon his true master and the real treasure of his life.

The precise amount of money, thirty pieces of silver, alludes to the Scriptures. In the allegory of Zechariah 11:4-17 the prophet becomes the good shepherd of God's flock which is being slaughtered by the false shepherds. The service of the good shepherd is valued at thirty pieces of silver, a paltry and insulting wage. It is the same sum, according to Exodus 21:31, which the owner of an ox had to give to the master of a slave if the slave had been gored. The mission of Jesus is appraised by the Jewish leaders, the false shepherds, at the same mean price. In both cases the money is thrown into the temple treasury, showing how shamefully God's loving care is requited.

These opening scenes form a prologue for the passion. Jesus has prophetically predicted his fate, has already been anointed for burial, and the plan of Judas has been set in motion. Everything that follows will be a playing-out of this prologue.

Matthew 26:17-19

> **Preparations for the Passover.** ¹⁷On the first day of the Feast of Unleavened Bread, the disciples approached Jesus and said, "Where do you want us to prepare for you to eat the Passover?" ¹⁸He said, "Go into the city to a certain man and tell him, 'The teacher says, "My appointed time draws near; in your house I shall celebrate the Passover with my disciples." ' " ¹⁹The disciples then did as Jesus had ordered, and prepared the Passover.

Matthew sharply abbreviates Mark's narrative here. While Mark emphasized Jesus' detailed foreknowledge, Matthew focuses on the clear commands of Jesus and the immediate response of his disciples in obedience. "The disciples did as Jesus had directed them" summarizes the type of discipleship that is a constant ideal throughout the Gospel.

Jesus' declaration, "my appointed time draws near," refers to the critical moment of his passion. This does not refer to chronological time, but to the climactic time toward which his entire life had been directed (8:29; 13:30; 21:34). All these references to "time" associate it with prophetic and apocalyptic references to the final age when God would bring definitive salvation to the world. Matthew makes clear that Jesus' death is the turning point of history, the new day of salvation.

Matthew 26:20-25

The Betrayer. [20]When it was evening, he reclined at table with the Twelve. [21]And while they were eating, he said, "Amen, I say to you, one of you will betray me." [22]Deeply distressed at this, they began to say to him one after another, "Surely it is not I, Lord?" [23]He said in reply, "He who has dipped his hand into the dish with me is the one who will betray me. [24]The Son of Man indeed goes, as it is written of him, but woe to that man by whom the Son of Man is betrayed. It would be better for that man if he had never been born." [25]Then Judas, his betrayer, said in reply, "Surely it is not I, Rabbi?" He answered, "You have said so."

The meal setting emphasizes the tragedy of Judas' betrayal. The meal, for the Jewish culture and many others, is a sign of unity, a celebration of friendship and family, and it is this sacred bond which Judas breaks.

The troubled questions of the disciples, "Surely it is not I, Lord?" remind Matthew's community that such temptation and betrayal is possible for anyone. All disciples must examine themselves, especially if they come to share in the trusting unity of the Eucharist.

Matthew adds here the title "Lord." He uses the title frequently for Jesus, especially when the disciples acknowledge his divine authority (8:2; 8:25; 12:8; 14:30). The disciples address Jesus as Lord here because they trust in his divine power. Judas, on the other hand, addresses Jesus as "Rabbi," a term of human respect often used of Jesus by unbelievers and his opponents. Judas will address Jesus again in Gethsemane with the same title of polite disbelief as he hands him over for arrest.

Matthew builds up Jesus' confrontation with the disciple when Judas asks, "Surely it is not I, Rabbi?," to which Jesus replies "You have said so." This is the same response Jesus will give to the high priest (26:64) and to Pilate (27:11) at his trial. In each case the burden is placed on the questioner and his own words condemn him. Each states the truth and Jesus' reply confirms that truth.

God's saving action and the sinful actions of people are intertwined in the passion accounts. Jesus' death is not simply the result of Judas' betrayal, but an inevitable fulfillment of prophecy. Yet Judas is responsible for his decision and must bear the consequences of his choice.

Matthew 26:26-30

The Lord's Supper. [26]While they were eating, Jesus took bread, said the blessing, broke it, and giving it to his disciples said, "Take and eat; this is my body." [27]Then he took a cup, gave thanks, and gave it to them, saying, "Drink from it, all of you, [28]for this is my blood of the covenant, which will be shed on behalf of many for the forgiveness of sins. [29]I tell you, from now on I shall not drink this fruit of the vine until the day when I drink it with you new in the kingdom of my Father." [30]Then, after singing a hymn, they went out to the Mount of Olives.

The institution of the Eucharist in Matthew's account is a slight modification of Mark's description and results in an even more liturgical account. It is easily detachable from the narrative unit surrounding it, since it is most likely part of a larger Eucharistic prayer. It is probably an accurate report of the way Matthew's community celebrated the Eucharist.

The narrative of the cup is transformed into a command, "Drink from it," to parallel the command, "Take and eat." The meal consists of ritual words and actions just as in the great Passover feast that the Jewish people were to commemorate over and over. Each time the meal is celebrated, the founding event is renewed and made present again.

Matthew focuses on the unity of Jesus and his disciples. In verse 26, Matthew replaces Mark's pronoun "he" with the name "Jesus," and the pronoun "them" with the noun "disciples." He inserts "with you" in verse 29 to show that the disciples will be united with Jesus to share in the final victory.

The words over the cup make it clear that this is the celebration of the covenant. Through his death Jesus becomes the blood bond between God and the people of God. Blood was considered the source of life, and the "blood of the covenant" was clearly drawn from Exodus 24 which narrates the ratifying of the covenant with Israel. This covenant in the blood of Jesus brings redemption as it is renewed in the Eucharistic celebration.

To the words over the cup Matthew adds, "for the forgiveness of sins." He has emphasized the ministry of forgiveness and reconciliation throughout his Gospel. Before his birth it was proclaimed, "he will save his people from their sins" (1:21). Jesus is continually referred to as the Suffering Servant who atones for the sins of the people. After his healings in chapter 8, the Servant Song (Isa 53) is quoted to show that he suffers for the sins of others (8:17). At the end of his third passion prediction Jesus explains that he comes "to give his life as a ransom for many" (20:28). When he is challenged at the healing of the paralytic, Jesus responds, "The Son of Man has authority on earth to forgive sins" (9:6). Jesus' words over the cup affirm that his death is the ultimate redeeming act, liberating humanity from the power of sin.

The covenant "for the forgiveness of sins" refers to the climactic prophecy of Jeremiah 31:31-34. Here God promises to establish a new covenant with the people. It will be open to all people and will be characterized by an internal law written on their hearts. Jesus establishes this new covenant in his blood and thus fulfills the promises made by the ancient prophets, to forgive the sins of his people and enter into a new relationship with humanity.

The Last Supper, like all previous Passover meals, is also a promise of hope. Jesus looks forward to the day when he will drink from the cup with his disciples in the Father's kingdom. The words of Jesus anticipate his death, "I shall not drink this fruit of the vine," but also look beyond his death to future glory. Matthew's account adds "with you" to point to Jesus' unity with his disciples in the future sharing of the kingdom.

Thus the Last Supper account is a prediction of Jesus' death and resurrection, and proclaims its meaning through rich biblical symbolism. The Passover, the covenant, forgiveness of sins, the Suffering Servant, the kingdom of God, all focus the readers' attention on the profound significance of Jesus' final acts. The hymns that were traditionally sung after the Passover, the "Hallel" (Pss. 114–118), give thanks to the Lord for constant faithfulness in redeeming God's people. With such faith on their lips, the disciples proceed with Jesus to the Mount of Olives.

Matthew 26:31-35

Peter's Denial Foretold. ³¹Then Jesus said to them, "This night all of you will have your faith in me shaken, for it is written:

'I will strike the shepherd,
and the sheep of the flock will be dispersed';

³²but after I have been raised up, I shall go before you to Galilee." ³³Peter said to him in reply, "Though all may have their faith in you shaken, mine will never be." ³⁴Jesus said to him, "Amen, I say to you, this very night before the cock crows, you will deny me three times." ³⁵Peter said to him, "Even though I should have to die with you, I will not deny you." And all the disciples spoke likewise.

The bond Jesus has established with his disciples is both affirmed and tested. The image of the shepherd and the sheep is repeated here to characterize that bond (9:36; 15:24). Matthew takes up the passage from Zechariah 13:7 that the shepherd will be struck and the sheep will be scattered. He adds the phrase "of the flock" to emphasize the community of disciples, the Church. Though his disciples will scatter like sheep after his arrest, Jesus assures them that after he is raised up, he will go like a shepherd before his sheep into Galilee.

Jesus shows the weakness in the bond of discipleship by saying, "all of you will have your faith in me shaken." Literally, the phrase reads, "all of you will be scandalized in me." The great danger to discipleship is to "stumble" in the face of the full meaning of his discipleship. They fall away at the prospect of the cross. All the disciples of Jesus flee because what is about to befall Jesus does not fit into their messianic hopes. Though Jesus has defined discipleship as taking up one's cross and following him (16:24), when the test comes, all will fall away.

In keeping with the special attention given to Peter in the Gospel, Matthew again shows the weakness of Peter in the midst of his determined character. At Caesarea Philippi the Gospel dramatizes Peter's rejection of the cross as unnecessary for Jesus' messiahship. Matthew alone records Peter's rebuke: "God forbid, Lord! No such thing shall ever happen to you" (16:23). In addition to Mark's recounting of Jesus' words, "Get behind me, Satan," Matthew adds, "You are an obstacle (scandal) to me" (16:23). There is a direct connection between the scene at Caesarea Philippi and this scene on the Mount of Olives. In both scenes Peter contradicts the prophetic words of Jesus. Just as Jesus calls Peter a "scandal" to him, Jesus will become a scandal to Peter as his faith is shaken. Peter refuses to consider the possibility of his own failure. Matthew makes Peter's determined fidelity more emphatic by adding "never" to Peter's statement that his faith will not be shaken.

Peter's final statement, "Even though I should have to die with you, I will not deny you," is a wonderful profession of what the personal bond of discipleship ought to be. However, Peter will exemplify the reality of failure for all future disciples. Peter, the first disciple called by Jesus (4:18), will be the last one to abandon him. Peter's confident insistence that he will never fail, is contrasted with his repeated denials of his discipleship when Jesus is on trial.

Matthew 26:36-46

The Agony in the Garden. ³⁶Then Jesus came with them to a place called Gethsemane, and he said to his disciples, "Sit here while I go over there and pray." ³⁷He took along Peter and the two sons of Zebedee, and began to feel sorrow and distress. ³⁸Then he said to them, "My soul is sorrowful even to death. Remain here and keep watch with me." ³⁹He advanced a little and fell prostrate in prayer, saying, "My Father, if it is possible, let this cup pass from me; yet, not as I will, but as you will." ⁴⁰When he returned to his disciples he found them asleep. He said to Peter, "So you could not keep watch with me for one hour? ⁴¹Watch and pray that you may not undergo the test. The spirit is willing, but the flesh is weak." ⁴²Withdrawing a second time, he prayed again, "My Father, if it is not possible that this cup pass without my drinking it, your will be done!" ⁴³Then he returned once more and found them asleep, for they could not keep their eyes open. ⁴⁴He left them and withdrew again and prayed a third time, saying the same thing again. ⁴⁵Then he returned to his disciples and said to them, "Are you still sleeping and taking your rest? Behold, the hour is at hand when the Son of Man is to be handed over to sinners. ⁴⁶Get up, let us go. Look, my betrayer is at hand."

The attention in this dramatic scene is not so much on the failure of the disciples, but on the prayer of Jesus. Throughout his Gospel, Matthew shows the prayer of Jesus as the model of prayer for the early Christian community. Where Mark places the emphasis on Jesus' threefold return to find the disciples asleep, Matthew highlights the threefold prayer of Jesus as he faithfully prepares for his arrest.

Jesus prays in the traditional, lamenting style of the Hebrews. Matthew says that Jesus felt sorrow and distress. He began to pray in the style of Psalm 42 which expresses a longing for God in the midst of great sorrow and distress. He then fell prostrate, literally "on the face," the reverential gesture of intense supplication.

The prayer of Jesus is more developed in Matthew's scene than in Mark's, and exemplifies the type of prayer Jesus had previously taught his disciples. He had given a model for prayer in the Lord's Prayer (6:9-13), and his prayer in Gethsemane echoes many elements of that prayer.

Jesus addresses God as "My Father," the title that continues the Father-Son metaphor used most often in Matthew (11:27). He not only prayed to God as Father, but he taught his disciples to understand God with the same intimate relationship (6:9).

Jesus' attention to the will of the Father in prayer echoes the third petition of the Our Father (6:10). Despite his very human fears and frailty, Jesus remains obedient. His conformity to the will of the Father becomes a model for all his followers as they face suffering and painful decisions.

The sixth petition of the Our Father (6:13) is exemplified as Jesus asks his disciples to pray that they may not undergo temptation (literally: "the test"). In both prayers the temptation does not so much refer to the occasional attractions of evil, but to the ultimate test. The Jewish apocalyptic writers referred to a period of severe trial before the end of the age, sometimes called the "messianic woes." This apocalyptic writing is exemplified in Matthew 24 as Jesus foretells the coming persecution and tribulation. The one who perseveres to the end will be saved as the commitment of the Christian community is tested.

Jesus gives a realistic explanation of the overwhelming nature of evil and why it is so easy to fall prey to it. The "spirit" and the "flesh" are the two struggling tendencies within each human person. The human spirit is fortified by God's Spirit and thus can remain faithful in trial. But the "flesh," human frailty and sinfulness, is too weak to be obedient under the test.

Jesus, through the obedience of his passion, is the exemplary model of faithfulness and prayer for the suffering Christian community. He remains watchful in prayer as the "hour" approaches. His readiness for the trial is strongly contrasted by the threefold return of Jesus to find his disciples sleeping. Throughout the Passion the contrasting attitudes of watchful obedience and drowsy unpreparedness will be played out.

Jesus triumphs in the face of trial and the disciples enter into temptation and flee.

Matthew 26:47-56

The Betrayal and Arrest of Jesus. ⁴⁷While he was still speaking, Judas, one of the Twelve, arrived, accompanied by a large crowd, with swords and clubs, who had come from the chief priests and the elders of the people. ⁴⁸His betrayer had arranged a sign with them, saying, "The man I shall kiss is the one; arrest him." ⁴⁹Immediately he went over to Jesus and said, "Hail, Rabbi!" and he kissed him. ⁵⁰Jesus answered him, "Friend, do what you have come for." Then stepping forward they laid hands on Jesus and arrested him. ⁵¹And behold, one of those who accompanied Jesus put his hand to his sword, drew it, and struck the high priest's servant, cutting off his ear. ⁵²Then Jesus said to him, "Put your sword back into its sheath, for all who take the sword will perish by the sword. ⁵³Do you think that I cannot call upon my Father and he will not provide me at this moment with more than twelve legions of angels? ⁵⁴But then how would the scriptures be fulfilled which say that it must come to pass in this way?" ⁵⁵At that hour Jesus said to the crowds, "Have you come out as against a robber, with swords and clubs to seize me? Day after day I sat teaching in the temple area, yet you did not arrest me. ⁵⁶But all this has come to pass that the writings of the prophets may be fulfilled." Then all the disciples left him and fled.

In keeping with his emphasis on the role of Judas, Matthew expands on the exchange between Jesus and his betrayer. Judas addresses him as "Rabbi," while in other passages true disciples address Jesus as "Lord." "Rabbi" is used only by Judas in Matthew and comes to indicate a faith response to Jesus that is far from complete. It is the same title used by Judas to question Jesus at the Last Supper: "Surely, it is not I, Rabbi?" (26:25).

Following the kiss of betrayal, Jesus responds to Judas. He addresses him as "friend," a polite but ironic salutation. "Do what you have come for" shows Jesus' command of the situation. He, in effect, gives permission for the final events to begin.

The incident of the sword is recounted very differently in Matthew. Mark vaguely refers to a bystander who cut off the ear of the high priest's slave. Presumably it was an accident as a result of the crowded mob scene. In Matthew it is one of the followers of Jesus who cut off the ear in a very deliberate reaction. The incident is followed by an extended teaching concerning violence and the will of the Father.

The violent reaction of a disciple provides the occasion for Jesus to reaffirm his non-violent stance. The force of the captors had provoked the violence of the disciple, a retaliatory response that Jesus clearly rejects. He orders the disciple to put his sword back in its sheath and proclaims, "all who take the sword will perish by the sword." By rejecting violence as self-destructive, Jesus is putting into practice what he taught in the Sermon on the Mount: "Offer no resistance to one who is evil" (5:39). "Love your enemies and pray for those who persecute you" (5:44).

Jesus also rejects the violent reaction because he does not need to be defended. If the Father willed to save Jesus by force, he would send legions of angels to do it. Jesus freely submits himself to the Father's will because the Scriptures must be fulfilled.

Only Matthew includes the detail of Jesus "sitting" in the temple. It emphasizes Matthew's portrayal of Jesus as the teacher of his Church. Throughout the Gospel, the sitting position expressed the authority of Jesus' teaching at the beginning of his major discourses (5:1; 13:1; 15:29).

Jesus concludes this section by explaining, "All this has come to pass that the writings of the prophets may be fulfilled." This designation of the Scriptures is unique to Matthew and fits the whole of his Gospel. All through the Gospel he has quoted from the prophets to show their fulfillment in the life of Jesus. He referred to the Scriptures as "the prophets and the law" (11:13) and he sees Jesus as the fulfillment of the Old Testament canon. Matthew understands the whole passion-resurrection as one climactic event that fulfills the prophecy of the Scriptures.

Matthew 26:57-68

Jesus before the Sanhedrin. [57]Those who had arrested Jesus led him away to Caiaphas the high priest, where the scribes and the elders were assembled. [58]Peter was following him at a distance as far as the high priest's courtyard, and going inside he sat down with the servants to see the outcome. [59]The chief priests and the entire Sanhedrin kept trying to obtain false testimony against Jesus in order to put him to death, [60]but they found none, though many false witnesses came forward. Finally two came forward [61]who stated, "This man said, 'I can destroy the temple of God and within three days rebuild it.' " [62]The high priest rose and addressed him, "Have you no answer? What are these men testifying against you?" [63]But Jesus was silent. Then the high priest said to him, "I order you to tell us under oath before the living God whether you are the Messiah, the Son of God." [64]Jesus said to him in reply, "You have said so. But I tell you:

From now on you will see 'the Son of Man
seated at the right hand of the Power'
and 'coming on the clouds of heaven.' "

[65]Then the high priest tore his robes and said, "He has blasphemed! What further need have we of witnesses? You have now heard the blasphemy; [66]what is your opinion?" They said in reply, "He deserves to die!" [67]Then they spat in his face and struck him, while some slapped him, [68]saying, "Prophesy for us, Messiah: who is it that struck you?"

The Jewish trial is taken from Mark's account, which presents it as a full, legal trial. Luke and John portray the event as only a hearing, leading to the full trial before Pilate. Matthew alone notes that the high priest was Caiaphas. The ruling assembly met in his home to pass judgment on Jesus.

Peter follows the crowd at a distance into the courtyard of Caiaphas. Matthew eliminates the colorful detail Mark gives about Peter warming himself by the fire. Instead, Matthew states Peter's purpose in being there: "to see the outcome." The word "outcome" has several meanings (end, result, goal) and, thus, the passage has several levels of meaning. Peter came to witness the result of the trial, the end of Jesus' life, and the goal toward which his whole life had been directed.

Matthew states clearly the illegitimacy of the trial and gives a consistently negative portrayal of the Jewish leaders. From the beginning he notes that the Sanhedrin's intention was to obtain false testimony so that Jesus could be put to death.

Mark says that the witnesses were false and did not agree. Matthew implies that the two witnesses are true as they both agree on Jesus' words. The words they attribute to Jesus are ironically true. Matthew changes Mark's "will destroy this temple" and "will build another" to "can destroy the temple and . . . rebuild it."

Jesus' messianic power extends to the temple itself. Jesus had stated his authority earlier in the Gospel: "I say to you, something greater than the temple is here" (12:6). The temple in Jerusalem would have already been destroyed (70 A.D.) at the time Matthew wrote his Gospel. The statement here by the witnesses is not so much about physical destruction, but about the messianic identity of Jesus.

The questions put to Jesus by the high priest concern Jesus' identity as "Christ" and "Son of God." Throughout the Gospel, Matthew has developed these titles to proclaim the true identity of Jesus. With the title "Christ," Matthew has shown Jesus to be Israel's Messiah, foretold by the prophets. "Son of God" makes clear the unique intimacy of Jesus with God, and his divine authority. Thus, the question of the high priest summarizes the major christological developments of the Gospel.

The high priest's question recalls the same titles of faith used in Peter's profession (16:16). Peter was able to affirm the identity of Jesus with partial faith, though he did not understand the necessity of suffering. The high priest asks his question in total disbelief and Jesus does not answer him directly because of the limited understanding of those titles. Jesus responds in the same way he responded to Judas (26:25): "You have said so."

The title "Son of Man" in Matthew is used to complement Jesus' suffering messiahship. The Son of Man sayings refer to the glorious reign of Jesus, his role as judge of the world, and his return in glory (10:23; 13:41; 16:27-28; 19:28; 24:30; 25:31). Just as Jesus' Son of Man identity completed Peter's profession of Jesus as Messiah and Son of God at Caesarea Philippi (16:27), here Jesus completes the high priest's question about his identity with a similar saying. Alluding to Psalm 110:1 and Daniel 7:13, Jesus speaks of the ultimate meaning of his death as leading to his glorification and exaltation.

Following the high priest's dramatic gesture, the Sanhedrin judges that Jesus deserves death. The prophet Jeremiah, who foreshadows the ministry and death of Jesus by his own life, was also judged worthy of death because he prophesied that the temple would be destroyed (Jer 26:8, 11). The Sanhedrin did not formally condemn Jesus during this night session. Matthew makes it clear that it was the Sanhedrin that began to mock Jesus as a false prophet. The mockery focuses on his messiahship, the central issue at the Jewish trial, while the Roman trial will condemn him for a political crime.

Matthew 26:69-75

Peter's Denial of Jesus. [69]Now Peter was sitting outside in the courtyard. One of the maids came over to him and said, "You too were with Jesus the Galilean." [70]But he denied it in front of everyone, saying, "I do not know what you are talking about!" [71]As he went out to the gate, another girl saw him and said to those who were there, "This man was with Jesus the Nazorean." [72]Again he denied it with an oath, "I do not know the man!" [73]A little later the bystanders came over and said to Peter, "Surely you too are one of them; even your speech gives you away." [74]At that he began to curse and to swear, "I do not know the man." And immediately a cock crowed. [75]Then Peter remembered the word that Jesus had spoken: "Before the cock crows you will deny me three times." He went out and began to weep bitterly.

Matthew adds drama to the account of Peter's denial of Jesus as the threefold denial gradually escalates in the scene. First, Peter claims that he does not know what the maid is talking about. Then, questioned by another girl, he explicitly denies that he knows Jesus. When the bystanders come over to accuse him, Peter begins to curse and swear as he denies any knowledge of Jesus.

The accusation made against Peter is that he was "with Jesus." The same phrase is used in other scenes to indicate the bond that existed between Jesus and his disciples. It is that affinity with Jesus, a relationship built up through many experiences, that Peter denies in his moment of weakness.

Matthew alone notes that Peter denies Jesus "in front of everyone." Throughout his Gospel, Matthew stresses the importance of public witness as an essential aspect of discipleship. In speaking of their mission, Jesus said: "Everyone who acknowledges me before others I will acknowledge before my heavenly Father. But whoever denies me before others, I will deny before my heavenly Father" (10:32-33). The proclamation of Jesus before the Sanhedrin is a strong contrast to the denial of Peter.

The cockcrow pierces this scene as it reaches a crescendo. The prediction of Jesus at the Last Supper and its fulfillment in Peter's denial is simplified by Matthew to a single cockcrow. Mark, with his characteristic attention to details, speaks of a second cockcrow. That haunting signal causes Peter to remember the prediction of Jesus and his own vehement statements of loyalty.

Given Peter's central role as spokesman for the disciples and rock of the Church in Matthew's Gospel, this scene takes on intense significance. It is an admonition to all future disciples, especially to leaders of the Church. Yet, in contrast to Judas, the experience of Peter offers hope. Peter wept bitterly at his failure and repented, while Judas despaired.

Matthew 27:1-2

Jesus before Pilate. ¹When it was morning, all the chief priests and the elders of the people took counsel against Jesus to put him to death. ²They bound him, led him away, and handed him over to Pilate, the governor.

The official decision to put Jesus to death is reached by the Sanhedrin in the morning, following an all-night trial. This decision is made more formal and deliberate in Matthew by emphasizing that it was reached after a long night of questioning and mockery. As Jesus is handed over to Pilate, the third passion prediction continues to be fulfilled: "The Son of Man will be handed over to the chief priests and the scribes, and they will condemn him to death, and hand him over to the Gentiles to be mocked and scourged and crucified" (20:18-19).

Pilate was prefect from 26 to 36 A.D. Matthew continually refers to him as the "governor," pointing to his political and military power. The title is a reminder of Jesus' words to his disciples as he spoke of their mission: "You will be led before governors and kings for my sake as a witness before them and the pagans" (10:18).

Matthew 27:3-10

The Death of Judas. ³Then Judas, his betrayer, seeing that Jesus had been condemned, deeply regretted what he had done. He returned the thirty pieces of silver to the chief priests and elders, ⁴saying, "I have sinned in betraying innocent blood." They said, "What is that to us? Look to it yourself." ⁵Flinging the money into the temple, he departed and went off and hanged himself. ⁶The chief priests gathered up the money, but said, "It is not lawful to deposit this in the temple treasury, for it is the price of blood." ⁷After consultation, they used it to buy the potter's field as a burial place for foreigners. ⁸That is why that field even today is called the Field of Blood. ⁹Then was fulfilled what had been said through Jeremiah the prophet, "And they took the thirty pieces of silver, the value of a man with a price on his head, a price set by some of the Israelites, ¹⁰and they paid it out for the potter's field just as the Lord had commanded me."

Matthew is the only evangelist to narrate the fate of Judas. Luke, in Acts 1:18-19, tells of a similar tradition, though with a number of differences. In both there is an explanation for the name "Field of Blood." In Matthew's Gospel the field is bought by the chief priests and the "blood" refers to the money used to purchase it. In Luke's version, Judas himself buys the field and spills his own blood upon it due to a fatal fall.

Seeing Jesus condemned to death, Judas deeply regrets his betrayal. Matthew deliberately avoids using the standard word for repentance, because Judas' regret was probably not a deep conversion of heart. Yet, Judas recognizes his mistake in betraying innocent blood and returns the thirty pieces of silver.

In predicting Judas' betrayal at the Last Supper, Jesus had expressed the tragedy of the crime: "Woe to that man by whom the Son of Man is betrayed. It would be better for that man if he had never been born" (26:24). Judas despairs and hangs himself. The deed is reminiscent of Ahithophel, betrayer of King David, who hanged himself after the crime (2 Sam 17:23).

Matthew characteristically alludes to the Old Testament to interpret the death of Judas and attributes the passage to Jeremiah. Yet it is actually a combination of several texts from both Zechariah and Jeremiah. Zechariah 11:13 speaks of the thirty pieces of silver thrown into the temple treasury. Several texts of Jeremiah speak of a potter's flask in the Valley of Ben-hinnom because there the people of Jersualem had worshipped false gods and spilled the blood of the innocent. The place is renamed the Valley of Slaughter and is made a burial place. Thus, the Field of Blood will be a sign of judgment upon Jerusalem because of the choices of Judas and the city's religious leaders to spill the blood of their innocent Messiah.

By showing us the last action taken by both Peter and Judas in the passion narrative, Matthew sets up a strong contrast. Peter "went out and began to weep bitterly," while Judas "went off and hanged himself." The failure of these two prominent disciples and their ultimate fate is both a warning and a message of hope to the future Church.

Matthew 27:11-14

Jesus Questioned by Pilate. [11]Now Jesus stood before the governor, and he questioned him, "Are you the king of the Jews?" Jesus said, "You say so." [12]And when he was accused by the chief priests and elders, he made no answer. [13]Then Pilate said to him, "Do you not hear how many things they are testifying against you?" [14]But he did not answer him one word, so that the governor was greatly amazed.

Following the insertion of Judas' suicide, Matthew continues the main line of narrative as Jesus is handed over to Pilate. The governor's opening question, "Are you the king of the Jews?" becomes the central question of the trial. The title "king of the Jews" is used only by the Gentiles in Matthew's Gospel. It was the title used by the Magi when they were looking for Jesus (2:2). It will be used again as the soldiers mock Jesus (27:29) and will be the inscription placed on the cross (27:37). To claim political kingship was treason against the Roman empire, a crime punishable by death.

Jesus' response, "You say so," is both an affirmation of its truth and a disassociation from the sense in which it was spoken. Jesus is the king, but not in the political sense which Pilate intended. Jesus used this same response to those who expressed the truth, but in a hostile and incomplete way: Judas (26:25) and the high priest (26:64).

Matthew stresses the silence of Jesus to all other charges. As he has throughout the Gospel, he associates Jesus with the Suffering Servant in chapter 53 of the Book of Isaiah. He bore his harsh treatment in silence and atoned for the sins of the people. Pilate's great amazement may also be a reference to the same Suffering Servant Song (Isa 52:14-15).

Matthew 27:15-26

The Sentence of Death. [15]Now on the occasion of the feast the governor was accustomed to release to the crowd one prisoner whom they wished. [16]And at that time they had a notorious prisoner called [Jesus] Barabbas. [17]So when they had assembled, Pilate said to them, "Which one do you want me to release to you, [Jesus] Barabbas, or Jesus called Messiah?" [18]For he knew that it was out of envy that they had handed him over. [19]While he was still seated on the bench, his wife sent him a message, "Have nothing to do with that righteous man. I suffered much in a dream today because of him." [20]The chief priests and the elders persuaded the crowds to ask for Barabbas but to destroy Jesus. [21]The governor said to them in reply, "Which of the two do you want me to release to you?" They answered, "Barabbas!" [22]Pilate said to them, "Then what shall I do with Jesus called Messiah?" They all said, "Let him be crucified!" [23]But he said, "Why? What evil has he done?" They only shouted the louder, "Let him be crucified!" [24]When Pilate saw that he was not succeeding at all, but that a riot was breaking out instead, he took water and washed his hands in the sight of the crowd, saying, "I am innocent of this man's blood. Look to it yourselves." [25]And the whole people said in reply, "His blood be upon us and upon our children." [26]Then he released Barabbas to them, but after he had Jesus scourged, he handed him over to be crucified.

The custom of releasing a prisoner at the feast of Passover was probably a concession to the Jews by the Romans. The nationalistic fever was high during the liberation feast and allowing them to choose a prisoner for release would cool their fervency. Matthew builds up this scene as the climactic choice in his passion narrative.

The preference of the people is made clear. Matthew makes several changes in and additions to Mark's Gospel to highlight that choice. A few ancient manuscripts read "Jesus Barabbas" in verses 16 and 17. Since Jesus was a common Jewish name it is probable that it was the original reading and then was later eliminated from the text out of respect for the name. The name Barabbas means "Son of the Father." Thus the contrast is obvious between Jesus Barabbas and Jesus the Messiah.

The choice is dramatized by Matthew's addition of the scene with Pilate's wife. She is ironically portrayed as a Gentile pleading the innocence of the Jewish Messiah. Just as the foreign Magi recognized Jesus in his infancy (2:2), Matthew continues to show that the Gentiles are more receptive to salvation than are the Jews. Reflecting the conflict of Christianity and Judaism in Matthew's community, these scenes lead to Jesus' final commission to "make disciples of all nations" (28:19).

The dream of Pilate's wife also recalls the many dreams in the infancy narrative. All of them are divine warnings about the fate of the Messiah. Joseph and the Magi heed those dreams and save the King of the Jews from those who sought to destroy him. This time the opportunity to save Jesus is lost as Pilate succumbs to the demands of the Jews.

Matthew focuses on the blame of the Jewish authorities and the dilemma of Pilate. He notes that it was out of envy the Jewish leaders handed Jesus over. It was the chief priests and elders who persuaded the crowds to choose Barabbas and to ask for Jesus' death. When Pilate asks what Jesus has done in order to establish his innocence, the crowds demand his death more vehemently. Matthew changes the shouts of the crowds from Mark's "Crucify him" to the passive "Let him be crucified," adding emphasis to the crowd's responsibility for the crucifixion. Pilate gave in to their demands only when he realized that he was not succeeding in convincing them of Jesus' innocence and that a riot was breaking out.

This whole section is tied together with the word "blood." Judas admits that he has betrayed innocent blood. The chief priests refer to the thirty pieces of silver as the price of blood and with the silver they purchase a field called the Field of Blood. Pilate declares that he is innocent of Jesus' blood and the people call down his blood upon themselves and their children.

Matthew is unique in recording the scene of Pilate's handwashing. This dramatic gesture seems to be drawn from an Old Testament practice (Deut 21:6-9). The symbolic gesture indicates one's innocence when human blood is unjustly shed, and is a plea to be absolved from guilt.

The dramatic response of the people is also unique to Matthew's Gospel and is important for the overall purpose of his Gospel. The words "his blood be upon us and upon our children" echoes Old Testament texts which express collective guilt for shedding innocent blood (Jer 26:15). The word "the crowd" is no longer used, but rather, "the whole people" which Matthew consistently uses to refer to the people of Israel for whom Jesus was sent.

Verse 25, often used as the excuse for vehement anti-Semitism through the centuries of Christianity, must be interpreted responsibly. The polemic reflects the hostility of Matthew's community and Pharisaic Judaism during the time of his writing. The responsibility for Jesus' blood fulfills the concluding words of Jesus in his woes upon the scribes and Pharisees: "there may come upon you all the righteous blood shed upon earth" (23:35). Matthew saw the Jewish War and the destruction of Jerusalem and the temple as a visible result of their fatal choice.

This evangelist's overall emphasis on the foundation of the Church shows that Israel's choice brings about the new people of God. Israel has lost the exclusive claim to be God's people; now that privilege would be given "to a people that will produce its fruit" (21:43). That new people is the Church composed of Jews and Gentiles.

Matthew 27:27-31

Mockery by the Soldiers. ²⁷Then the soldiers of the governor took Jesus inside the praetorium and gathered the whole cohort around him. ²⁸They stripped off his clothes and threw a scarlet military cloak about him. ²⁹Weaving a crown out of thorns, they placed it on his head, and a reed in his right hand. And kneeling before him, they mocked him, saying, "Hail, King of the Jews!" ³⁰They spat upon him and took the reed and kept striking him on the head. ³¹And when they had mocked him, they stripped him of the cloak, dressed him in his own clothes, and led him off to crucify him.

After the trial before the Sanhedrin, Jesus was mocked and ridiculed as the Messiah. Now after the trial before Pilate, Jesus is derided as the King of the Jews. The derision and torment of Jesus is a cruel and ironic preparation for the crucifixion.

Matthew heightens the motif of kingship. The scarlet robe replaces Mark's purple cloak, the color worn by the emperor, and is probably more historical since scarlet was the outer cloak worn by the ordinary Roman soldier. The thorns were shaped to resemble a royal diadem. Matthew also adds a reed to mockingly imitate a royal scepter.

The scene gradually builds from derision to abuse and violence. The brutality of the scene is in direct contrast to the non-violent teachings of Jesus. Jesus taught his followers not to retaliate and he follows his own teaching as he submits to the violence against him.

The mockery of Jesus as King of the Jews, just as the accusation at his trial, ironically proclaims the truth of who he is. As his tormentors kneel before him and hail him as king, the reader knows that he is a king in a manner totally different from earthly expectations. He is the king who is "meek and riding on an ass" (21:5), the king who "will sit upon his royal throne and all the nations will be assembled before him" (25:31-32).

Matthew 27:32-44

The Way of the Cross. ³²As they were going out, they met a Cyrenian named Simon; this man they pressed into service to carry his cross.

The Crucifixion. ³³And when they came to a place called Golgotha (which means Place of the Skull), ³⁴they gave Jesus wine to drink mixed with gall. But when he had tasted it, he refused to drink.

³⁵After they had crucified him, they divided his garments by casting lots; ³⁶then they sat down and kept watch over him there. ³⁷And they placed over his head the written charge against him: This is Jesus, the King of the Jews. ³⁸Two revolutionaries were crucified with him, one on his right and the other on his left. ³⁹Those passing by reviled him, shaking their heads ⁴⁰and saying, "You who would destroy the temple and rebuild it in three days, save yourself, if you are the Son of God, [and] come down from the cross!" ⁴¹Likewise the chief priests with the scribes and elders mocked him and said, ⁴²"He saved others; he cannot save himself. So he is the king of Israel! Let him come down from the cross now, and we will believe in him. ⁴³He trusted in God; let him deliver him now if he wants him. For he said, 'I am the Son of God.'" ⁴⁴The revolutionaries who were crucified with him also kept abusing him in the same way.

Because criminals could not be executed within the walls of the holy city, Jesus was taken outside Jerusalem to a small hill called Golgotha. The details about the family of Simon of Cyrene are omitted, probably because his family was not known to Matthew's community. Matthew makes the reference to Psalm 69:22 more explicit by changing Mark's "wine drugged with myrrh" to "wine mixed with gall," a bitter and poisonous extract. The garments of an executed man fell to the executioners, and the Gospel includes this incident as a fulfillment of Psalm 22:19. The act of crucifixion is noted almost as an aside, while the incidental details are accented to show how the whole event fulfills the Scriptures.

The inscription on the cross, written above the head of Jesus, is expanded by Matthew: "This is Jesus, the King of the Jews." Matthew often substitutes the name of Jesus for Mark's pronouns. Jesus' name becomes more significant, especially since Matthew had interpreted that name early in his Gospel: "You are to name him Jesus, because he will save his people from their sins" (1:21). Again, the title "King of the Jews" becomes an ironic proclamation of the truth. The two revolutionaries, one on his right and the other on his left, become his royal court.

The mockery of Jesus on the cross essentially follows the form in Mark. He is derided first by the passersby who mock the power he claimed over the temple. Next, the Jewish leaders ridicule him as king of Israel. Finally, the two crucified on either side of Jesus revile him, but their words are not reported.

61

Matthew's Gospel adds significantly to this section as he weaves in the transcendent title, Son of God. He adds to the first mockery: "If you are the Son of God, come down from the cross." This condition echoes the challenge of the demon in the desert (4:3-9). Each of the mocking temptations was designed to turn Jesus aside from his mission. Now instead of being asked to turn stones into bread or throw himself down from the temple or worship Satan, he is asked to "come down from the cross."

The final words of mockery are also unique to Matthew: "He trusted in God; let God deliver him now if God wants him. For he said, 'I am the Son of God.'" The words combine two scriptural quotations; the first part is a citation of Psalm 22:9 and the whole quotation reflects Wisdom 2:18-20. In Wisdom 2, the just one claims to be God's son and so is condemned to a shameful death. His foes test him to see if God will defend and rescue him.

This addition of the Son of God passages fits well into Matthew's plan. Jesus had been revealed as Son of God in his infancy (2:15), at his baptism (3:17), and at the transfiguration (17:5). The disciples proclaimed him as Son of God while in the boat, and Peter professed him as Son of the living God at Caesarea Philippi. A crucified Son of God is impossible for all to accept, and the taunt of the Jewish leaders was the final test of Jesus' divine sonship. What seems like convincing proof that Jesus is not God's son becomes, in Matthew, the ultimate proof as Jesus trusts and obeys until the end.

Matthew 27:45-56

The Death of Jesus. [45]From noon onward, darkness came over the whole land until three in the afternoon. [46]And about three o'clock Jesus cried out in a loud voice, *"Eli, Eli, lema sabachthani?"* which means, "My God, my God, why have you forsaken me?" [47]Some of the bystanders who heard it said, "This one is calling for Elijah." [48]Immediately one of them ran to get a sponge; he soaked it in wine, and putting it on a reed, gave it to him to drink. [49]But the rest said, "Wait, let us see if Elijah comes to save him." [50]But Jesus cried out again in a loud voice, and gave up his spirit. [51]And behold, the veil of the sanctuary was torn in two from top to bottom. The earth quaked, rocks were split, [52]tombs were opened, and the bodies of many saints who had fallen asleep were raised. [53]And coming forth from their tombs after his resurrection, they entered the holy city and appeared to many. ⁵⁴The centurion and the men with him who were keeping watch over Jesus feared greatly when they saw the earthquake and all that was happening, and they said, "Truly, this was the Son of God!" ⁵⁵There were many women there, looking on from a distance, who had followed Jesus from Galilee, ministering to him. ⁵⁶Among them were Mary Magdalene and Mary the mother of James and Joseph, and the mother of the sons of Zebedee.

As in all the Gospel accounts, physical aspects of Jesus' suffering and death are recounted briefly and factually with little comment. The emphasis is on the meaning of these events and their correspondence with the Scriptures. Matthew expands upon the events that accompany Jesus' death in order to focus on the central themes of his passion account.

The darkness that covered the land is a common prophetic and apocalyptic motif expressing divine judgment on the Day of the Lord (Amos 8:9). Matthew's remark that it covered "all" the land points to its additional allusion to the ninth plague which preceded Israel's deliverance.

The cry of Jesus from the cross is a quotation of the first words of Psalm 22. But where Mark quotes Jesus' words in Aramaic ("Eloi, Eloi"), Matthew quotes the words in Hebrew, "Eli, Eli," which means, "my God, my God." The change makes clearer the reason for the confusion of the crowds as they think Jesus is calling on Elijah. Since Elijah was believed to come to the help of those in distress, and since his name is derived from the same Hebrew word as Eli, the confusion seems understandable.

Matthew subtly changes Mark's stark description of Jesus' last moment. The verb "cried out" is the same word repeatedly used in Psalm 22 and other laments to describe a person voicing a desperate prayer. Jesus "gave up his spirit," emphasizing his control over his destiny and his obedient giving up of his life.

The events following Jesus' death help to interpret the meaning of his death. With the exception of the tearing of the veil of the sanctuary, the miraculous signs are a unique contribution of Matthew and reflect his interest in the fulfillment of Scripture. The earthquake, opening of the tombs, the resurrection, and appearance of the saints are all the type of apocalyptic events prophesied for the end of the age.

In the Old Testament the quaking of the earth signals God's presence and power being made known. In his apocalyptic discourse Jesus speaks of earthquakes as one of the signs marking "the beginning of the labor pains" (24:8). It is a common sign in Jewish literature to show the shaking of the old world and the breaking in of God's kingdom.

The earthquake leads to the splitting of the rocks and the liberation of the holy ones from their rock tombs. The resurrection of the dead marks the beginning of the new age begun by the death and resurrection of Jesus. The opening of the graves alludes to the prophecy of Ezekiel: "Then you shall know that I am the Lord, when I open your graves and have you rise from them" (Ezek 37:13). The resurrection marks a new beginning and a recognition of God's presence.

The saints who were raised represent the holy ones of the Old Testament. Although the death and resurrection of Jesus brings forth a new people, God does not forsake the saints of Israel. Matthew makes clear that the resurrection of Jesus precedes the appearance of the saints in Jerusalem.

The climactic confession of Christian faith is made not only by the centurion, as in Mark's account, but by those with him keeping watch over Jesus. Since the disciples had already confessed that Jesus is the Son of God, Matthew makes it clear that this is the opening of faith to the Gentiles. Again Psalm 22 influences the final scene as Matthew shows the scope of the salvation won by Jesus: "All the ends of the earth shall remember and turn to the Lord; all the families of the nations shall bow down before him" (Ps 22:28).

Matthew 27:57-61

The Burial of Jesus. [57]When it was evening, there came a rich man from Arimathea named Joseph, who was himself a disciple of Jesus. [58]He went to Pilate and asked for the body of Jesus; then Pilate ordered it to be handed over. [59]Taking the body, Joseph wrapped it [in] clean linen [60]and laid it in his new tomb that he had hewn in the rock. Then he rolled a huge stone across the entrance to the tomb and departed. [61]But Mary Magdalene and the other Mary remained sitting there, facing the tomb.

Matthew abbreviates the account of the burial but gives a few additional details. He does not call Joseph "a distinguished member of the council," probably to disassociate him from the trial of Jesus. Instead, Matthew adds that Joseph of Arimathea was a rich man, and he was a disciple of Jesus.

The details added by Matthew show the devotion of Joseph, who remained faithful to Jesus at the end. Only Matthew notes that the shroud was made of clean linen, that the tomb was new, and that it was personally owned by Joseph. The women, too, remain faithful followers, taking up their silent vigil facing the tomb.

The scene, as in Mark's account, prepares for the drama of the resurrection. Matthew adds that the stone that closed the entrance to the tomb was huge. The fact that the tomb had recently been cut from the rock and was known to be owned by a prominent person distinguishes it from all the many tombs around Jerusalem. And the fact that the same two women who will see the empty tomb also saw the precise place where Jesus' body was laid is a defense of the reality of the resurrection.

Matthew 27:62-66

The Guard at the Tomb. ⁶²The next day, the one following the day of preparation, the chief priests and the Pharisees gathered before Pilate ⁶³and said, "Sir, we remember that this imposter while still alive said, 'After three days I will be raised up.' ⁶⁴Give orders, then, that the grave be secured until the third day, lest his disciples come and steal him and say to the people, 'He has been raised from the dead.' This last imposture would be worse than the first." ⁶⁵Pilate said to them, "The guard is yours; go secure it as best you can." ⁶⁶So they went and secured the tomb by fixing a seal to the stone and setting the guard.

This final scene before the resurrection narrative is found only in Matthew's Gospel. It reflects the controversy that raged between Jews and Christians in Matthew's community and through most of Israel in the first century. The two groups had radically different explanations for the empty tomb. The Jews explained the resurrection as a hoax by charging that the disciples had stolen the body of Jesus from the tomb. Christians proclaimed it as an act of God's vindication and triumph. Matthew wants to assure his readers that Jesus' body had not been stolen since the Jews themselves sealed the tomb and set a guard over it.

The chief priests and Pharisees call Jesus an "imposter," a description not previously given to him in the Gospel. They recall Jesus' prophecy, repeated three times in the Gospel, that he would be raised up after three days. Their fear that his disciples would proclaim, "He has been raised from the dead," is an anticipation of what would become the core of early Christian preaching. Their worry that "this last imposter would be worse than the first" ironically hints at the explosive proclamation that would break forth following Jesus' resurrection.

The scene with Pilate recalls the Roman trial. Again Pilate gives in to their demands, yet he leaves it to the Jewish leaders to carry out their own wishes. Pilate, who allowed the crucifixion of Jesus only after declaring his own innocence, now mockingly tells them to "go secure it as best you can." The statement ironically prepares for the resurrection scenes since no matter how securely the tomb was guarded, they could not prevent the victorious resurrection.

Matthew 28:1-10

The Resurrection of Jesus. ¹After the sabbath, as the first day of the week was dawning, Mary Magdalene and the other Mary came to see the tomb. ²And behold, there was a great earthquake; for an angel of the Lord descended from heaven, approached, rolled back the stone, and sat upon it. ³His appearance was like lightning and his clothing was white as snow. ⁴The guards were shaken with fear of him and became like dead men. ⁵Then the angel said to the women in reply, "Do not be afraid! I know that you are seeking Jesus the crucified. ⁶He is not here, for he has been raised just as he said. Come and see the place where he lay. ⁷Then go quickly and tell his disciples, 'He has been raised from the dead, and he is going before you to Galilee; there you will see him.' Behold, I have told you." ⁸Then they went away quickly from the tomb, fearful yet overjoyed, and ran to announce this to his disciples. ⁹And behold, Jesus met them on their way and greeted them. They approached, embraced his feet, and did him homage. ¹⁰Then Jesus said to them, "Do not be afraid. Go tell my brothers to go to Galilee, and there they will see me."

The accounts of the resurrection in the four Gospels differ significantly. While the fact that Jesus was raised from the dead was the core of early Christian preaching, a description of the details and circumstances of the resurrection and appearances was not a part of the earliest preaching tradition. Aside from certain basic facts, each of the evangelists adds his own peculiar traditions and culminates the unique message of the Gospel in the resurrection account.

Matthew mentions only two women who came to the tomb. They are the same women who faithfully remained with Jesus at his death and stood watching the tomb at his burial (27:61). Since Matthew states that the tomb was sealed and guarded by soldiers, he cannot say that the women came to anoint Jesus' body. Rather, they came "to see the tomb," to resume their faithful vigil of mourning.

The apocalyptic events which interpreted the death of Jesus continue in the resurrection accounts. The details are characteristic descriptions of the end time in Jewish literature, and through them Matthew ties the death and resurrection into one great final event. Again the earthquake proclaims the shaking of the old world to its foundations and the beginning of the new and decisive age of salvation.

The angel, as messenger of God in Jewish and early Christian writings, manifests the words and deeds of God. The angel descended from heaven, rolled back the stone, and sat upon it in triumph. Matthew shows that the resurrection is a divine action, the vindication of Jesus as God triumphs over death in the resurrection of the Son.

The message of the angel is typical of a theophany, a manifestation of God's presence, and hearkens back to the angelic messages at the beginning of the Gospel. In contrast to the deadening fear of the guards, the angel tells the women, "Do not be afraid." The message of the angel proclaims the meaning of the empty tomb. "Jesus the crucified" is not in the place of death, but as the core of Christian preaching proclaimed, "He has been raised." The addition in Matthew, "just as he said," recalls Jesus' confidence in his victory over death. Each of his passion predictions included a prediction of resurrection (16:21; 17:23; 20:19).

The angel then gives the women a mission: "Go quickly." They are to proclaim the message of the resurrection to the disciples and to remind them of Jesus' promise (26:32) that he will go before them to Galilee where they will see him. The reaction of the women, "fearful yet overjoyed," is the typical and paradoxical reaction to divine manifestation throughout the Scriptures. In contrast to the silencing fear of the women in Mark's account, they ran quickly to announce the good news to the disciples.

The appearance of the risen Jesus to the women is unique in Matthew, though there are similarities to his appearance to Mary of Magdala in John 20:14-18. As Jesus met them with the usual Greek term of greeting, the women grasped his feet and worshiped him. The scene shows that the risen presence of Jesus is a real body which can be grasped, affirming the oneness of the earthly and risen Jesus.

Jesus does not allow the women to linger in adoration, but encourages them on their mission. The commission of Jesus to the women is basically the same as that given to them by the angel, except Jesus calls the disciples "my brothers." This indicates his forgiveness of the disciples for their failure and his restoration of them to full fellowship with him. He urges the women to continue on their mission of evangelization, the mission to which he will call all of his disciples as the Gospel draws to a close.

Matthew 28:11-15

The Report of the Guard. [11]While they were going, some of the guard went into the city and told the chief priests all that had happened. [12]They assembled with the elders and took counsel; then they gave a large sum of money to the soldiers, [13]telling them, "You are to say, 'His disciples came by night and stole him while we were asleep.' [14]And if this gets to the ears of the governor, we will satisfy [him] and keep you out of trouble." [15]The soldiers took the money and did as they were instructed. And this story has circulated among the Jews to the present [day].

This incident, reported only by Matthew, shows the result of posting a guard at the tomb (27:62-66). Having failed to prevent the resurrection, the Jewish leaders now try to render it unbelievable. They explain the resurrection as a theft of the body by the disciples, the prevention of which was the very reason the guard had been posted.

The scene is reminiscent of the gathering that began the passion account. There, too, the chief priests and elders took counsel to put an end to Jesus and they used money to achieve their purpose. Here the Jewish leaders bribe the soldiers with money in order to put an end to the resurrection story.

This story that "has circulated among the Jews to the present day" was one encountered in the Church of Matthew's time. It was an attempt to refute the explanation of the empty tomb proclaimed by the Christians. It should be read in light of the arguments between the Church and synagogue of the first century.

Matthew 28:16-20

The Commissioning of the Disciples. [16]The eleven disciples went to Galilee, to the mountain to which Jesus had ordered them.

¹⁷When they saw him, they worshiped, but they doubted. ¹⁸Then Jesus approached and said to them, "All power in heaven and on earth has been given to me. ¹⁹Go, therefore, and make disciples of all nations, baptizing them in the name of the Father, and of the Son, and of the holy Spirit, ²⁰teaching them to observe all that I have commanded you. And behold, I am with you always, until the end of the age."

Matthew culminates several major themes of the Gospel in this final scene. The eleven disciples had received the message of the women and gathered in Galilee. They assemble on a mountain, the setting for special revelation throughout the Gospel (5:1; 14:23; 15:29; 17:1). At the beginning of Jesus' ministry the devil took him to a very high mountain and tempted him to establish a worldly kingdom. Now, Jesus receives all power in heaven and earth from the Father.

The phrase "when they saw him" is the only reference Matthew makes to Jesus' resurrection appearance to the disciples. Their response to Jesus seems paradoxical. They worship him, yet they doubt. "Doubt" here implies weakness in faith or hesitation. The verb is unique to Matthew's Gospel and is used to refer to Peter's hesitant faith as he walked on the turbulent waters. This mixture of faith and uncertainty is shown to be characteristic of Christian discipleship until the close of the age.

Because the power and authority of Jesus is now made universal by his death and resurrection, Jesus commissions his disciples to a worldwide mission. The limitations of his ministry (15:24) and the restrictions he places upon the mission of the disciples, a mission only to "the lost sheep of the house of Israel" (10:6), are now overcome. Because Jesus gave his life "for the many," the fruits of his death are now offered to all people, Jews and Gentiles.

Baptism expresses the incorporation of a believer into the life of God and the Church. The trinitarian formula of baptism became the liturgical tradition of the Church and expresses the effects of baptism, union with the Father, Son, and Holy Spirit. Jesus' own baptism is described as a trinitarian scene (3:16-17) and both scenes reflect the developed belief in the divinity of the Son and Holy Spirit in Matthew's Church.

Because of Matthew's strong ecclesial interest, the commissioning of the disciples reflects the threefold mission of the Church: evangelization, baptism, and teaching. The initial task is the proclamation of the good news. Then new disciples are brought into the life of the

Church through baptism. Finally, detailed teaching in the way of Christ must guide the new disciples.

The closing verse of Matthew assures the Church of the abiding presence of Jesus as the disciples take up their mission. At the beginning of the Gospel, Matthew announced that Jesus is Emmanuel, "God is with us" (1:23). That same personal presence of God will be always with the disciples to give them confidence as they await the final coming of Jesus in glory.

The Passion and Resurrection According to Luke

Luke's account of the passion relies on Mark as its principal source, yet it differs from Mark in significant ways. There are many incidents in Mark's Gospel that have been omitted in Luke, and new material added that is not found in Mark. Strangely, many of the details that diverge from Mark are very similar to those found in John's Gospel. Obviously Luke was familiar with traditions of the passion other than that found in Mark. In addition, Luke's sequence of events often differs from the order used by Mark as Luke uses his sources creatively to highlight his own unique themes.

Luke is also the author of the Acts of the Apostles, the second part of his two-volume work. Therefore, when interpreting the Gospel, it is most helpful to analyze it within the context of both works. Acts is not only the completion of the Gospel, but the Church in Acts influences the shape of Luke's Gospel. The passion and resurrection of Jesus as the climactic events of the Gospel are also the fountainhead from which flows the life of the early Church.

Jesus is depicted in his passion as the innocent sufferer. Pilate declares Jesus innocent three times during his trial. Where the Gentile centurion in Mark professed Jesus' identity, the centurion in Luke declares that Jesus is surely innocent. Jesus sets the example for all future martyrs of the Church who will suffer in innocence to give witness to Jesus. Throughout Acts, his disciples follow his example in their trials.

Throughout the passion Jesus remains concerned for the needs of others as he had all through his life. He shows compassion as he heals the ear of the high priest's slave, and shows concern for the fate of the women along the road. The forgiving mercy demonstrated during his ministry continues as he forgives his executioners and promises paradise to the repentant thief. When he appears to his disciples after his resurrection he commissions them to extend his work of forgiveness to all the nations. The content of their preaching is to be "repentance for the forgiveness of sins."

The journey of Jesus toward Jerusalem is a distinctive aspect of Luke's Gospel that gives it a sense of purpose and direction. The journey includes every aspect of Jesus' passion, death, resurrection, and ascension. Ultimately it is his journey to the Father. The city of Jesus' destiny becomes the place of fulfillment. There in Jerusalem Jesus accomplishes his "exodus." As Jesus ascends to the Father, Jerusalem becomes the place of the Spirit's empowerment of the Church and the place from which the disciples would extend their witness.

The disciples journeying to Emmaus learn to recognize Jesus through his word and sacrament; they continue the journey of Jesus to all the world, even to the ends of the earth.

Luke 22:1-6

The Conspiracy against Jesus. [1]Now the feast of Unleavened Bread, called the Passover, was drawing near, [2]and the chief priests and the scribes were seeking a way to put him to death, for they were afraid of the people. [3]Then Satan entered into Judas, the one surnamed Iscariot, who was counted among the Twelve, [4]and he went to the chief priests and temple guards to discuss a plan for handing him over to them. [5]They were pleased and agreed to pay him money. [6]He accepted their offer and sought a favorable opportunity to hand him over to them in the absence of a crowd.

Like the other Gospel writers, Luke sets the scene for the passion narrative at the time of Passover. Originating as separate feasts, Passover and the Feast of Unleavened Bread are now celebrated as a unit. Luke has prepared his readers to understand Jesus' passion as a new event of liberation. At the Transfiguration, Moses and Elijah spoke of the "exodus" Jesus was going to accomplish in Jerusalem (9:30).

Luke introduces a new protagonist into the plot to destroy Jesus. In addition to the chief priests, the scribes, and Judas, he speaks of the role of Satan. Judas' role in the conspiracy is credited to Satan's entry into him. Satan's role here had been prepared for during the temptations in the desert. After failing in his mission to overcome Jesus, the devil had "departed from him for a time" (4:13). The passion becomes the opportune time for Satan to assault Jesus and his followers. Luke, who had referred to the apostolic mission as the fall of Satan from the sky (10:18), now presents the passion accounts as Jesus' great confrontation with the forces of evil.

Luke 22:7-13

Preparations for the Passover. ⁷When the day of the Feast of Unleavened Bread arrived, the day for sacrificing the Passover lamb, ⁸he sent out Peter and John, instructing them, "Go and make preparations for us to eat the Passover." ⁹They asked him, "Where do you want us to make the preparations?" ¹⁰And he answered them, "When you go into the city, a man will meet you carrying a jar of water. Follow him into the house that he enters ¹¹and say to the master of the house, 'The teacher says to you, "Where is the guest room where I may eat the Passover with my disciples?" ' ¹²He will show you a large upper room that is furnished. Make the preparations there." ¹³Then they went off and found everything exactly as he had told them, and there they prepared the Passover.

In describing the preparations for the Passover meal, Luke places emphasis on the initiative of Jesus. Whereas in Matthew and Mark the disciples ask Jesus where they should prepare the Passover, here Jesus commands two of the Twelve, Peter and John, to prepare for the meal. Jesus is shown as firmly in control of the events about to transpire.

Luke also shows that the meal was not the Passover of Jesus alone. Jesus instructs Peter and John, "Go and make preparations for us to eat the Passover," and thus includes the disciples in the events that will take place. All followers of Jesus will share in the events of liberation, the Passover from death to life.

Luke 22:14-20

The Last Supper. ¹⁴When the hour came, he took his place at table with the apostles. ¹⁵He said to them, "I have eagerly desired to eat this Passover with you before I suffer, ¹⁶for, I tell you, I shall not eat it [again] until there is fulfillment in the kingdom of God." ¹⁷Then he took a cup, gave thanks, and said, "Take this and share it among yourselves; ¹⁸for I tell you [that] from this time on I shall

73

not drink of the fruit of the vine until the kingdom of God comes." [19]Then he took the bread, said the blessing, broke it, and gave it to them, saying, "This is my body, which will be given for you; do this in memory of me." [20]And likewise the cup after they had eaten, saying, "This cup is the new covenant in my blood, which will be shed for you.

Luke's account of the Last Supper differs significantly from Mark's and Matthew's narratives. It is Jesus' final historical meal with his disciples before its fulfillment in the kingdom of God. Thus the meal has the characteristics of a farewell banquet as Jesus prepares the disciples for his death and for their future.

Luke includes many elements of the farewell discourse of other writings. The Old Testament contains the farewell speeches of Jacob (Gen 47–50), Joshua (Josh 23–24), Moses (Deut 31–34), and David (1 Kgs 2:1–10). The genre is carried over into the New Testament where it is found in John 13–17, the Pastoral Letters, and in Luke's writing (Acts 20). In such discourses the leader assembles his successors and tells them of his imminent death. He retraces the course of his own life and prepares them for the future. The leader exhorts his followers in right conduct and commissions them for their mission.

More than any other evangelist, Luke shows meals to be the context out of which Jesus teaches his disciples. Such meals were always inclusive events, scandalizing those around him. Gentiles, prostitutes, tax collectors, sinners, as well as the blind, the lame, and the poor were invited to share his table fellowship. At these meals Jesus taught his disciples the table virtues of hospitality, service, humility, and concern for the poor.

Verses 15–17 are unique to Luke. Jesus foretells his coming suffering and death and tells his apostles that this will be his last meal with them. Yet Jesus also gives a future dimension to the Passover meal by his reference to the kingdom of God. The Passover meal, which Jesus will never eat again, will find its fulfillment in the banquet of God's kingdom.

The first cup of wine is a traditional part of the Passover meal. It is not the cup of the Eucharist referred to in verse 20. The future orientation of verse 18 parallels that of verse 16. Both speak of the finality of this meal, but they likewise predict the future triumph of Jesus. The kingdom of God will be established with his death and resurrection.

The Eucharistic narration of verses 19 and 20 reflect the liturgy of Luke's community. The tradition recorded here is closest to that cited by Paul in 1 Corinthians 11:23–26. The words over the bread and over the cup reinterpret the elements of the Passover meal in terms of Jesus. Luke makes it clear that Jesus offers himself to his disciples. Luke's addition of "which will be given for you" and "which will be shed for you" gives greater salvific significance to Jesus' death.

Luke's narration emphasizes that the cup is the "new covenant" established by the shedding of the blood of Jesus. The words recall not only the blood of the covenant sprinkled by Moses on Sinai, but also the "new covenant" announced in Jeremiah 31:31.

As in Paul's letter to the people of Corinth, Luke's tradition adds the directive, "Do this in memory of me." Like the ancient Passover, the ritual meal is not a mere recollection of Jesus, but a representation of him and his saving acts. The disciples are directed to continue doing what Jesus has done, both in a ritual sense and a lived sense through self-giving.

Luke 22:21-23

> **The Betrayal Foretold.** ²¹"And yet behold, the hand of the one who is to betray me is with me on the table; ²²for the Son of Man indeed goes as it has been determined; but woe to that man by whom he is betrayed." ²³And they began to debate among themselves who among them would do such a deed.

In Mark and Matthew the announcement of the betrayal occurs before the institution of the Eucharist. By placing it after the event Luke creates a sharp contrast between the self-giving actions of Jesus and the selfishness of the betrayer. The treachery is heightened by noting that the betrayer's hand is on the Passover table.

As the disciples debate among themselves over who would do such a deed, Luke is telling future disciples that their presence at the Eucharist is no assurance of fidelity to Jesus. The betrayal is part of the divine necessity of Jesus' suffering, yet the personal responsibility of the betrayer is not diminished. In fact, the responsibility is greater because he was one of Jesus' intimate friends.

Luke 22:24-30

> **The Role of the Disciples.** ²⁴Then an argument broke out among them about which of them should be regarded as the greatest. ²⁵He

> said to them, "The kings of the Gentiles lord it over them and those in authority over them are addressed as 'Benefactors'; [26]but among you it shall not be so. Rather, let the greatest among you be as the youngest, and the leader as the servant. [27]For who is greater: the one seated at table or the one who serves? Is it not the one seated at table? I am among you as the one who serves. [28]It is you who have stood by me in my trials; [29]and I confer a kingdom on you, just as my Father has conferred one on me, [30]that you may eat and drink at my table in my kingdom; and you will sit on thrones judging the twelve tribes of Israel.

After arguing among themselves about who is the worst apostle, the disciples begin to quarrel over who is the greatest. Such disputes among them provide an opportunity for Jesus to address them on true apostolic leadership and how such leadership is to be exercised.

A scene similar to this one occurs in Mark and Matthew. There the scene is placed before the passion narrative and is occasioned by the request of James and John for seats at Jesus' right and left in his glory (Mark 10:42-45; Matt 20:25-28). In the Lukan setting, the dispute involves all the apostles and is concerned with greatness in the present. By placing Jesus' words within the context of the meal, Luke reminds the Church that the Eucharist must always lead to service of others. In this, Luke is similar to John who shows Jesus taking up the role of a servant and washing his disciples' feet while sharing the meal and speaking of his betrayer (John 13).

Jesus first points to the authority and titles of earthly rulers. He reverses the worldly order of human relationships, and points to his own life of service as an example of such a relationship. Those who are truly great are those who serve in imitation of him. Such advice occurs throughout Luke's Gospel, beginning with the Magnificat where the proud and mighty are brought low and the lowly are exalted (1:51-53). In 14:11 and 18:14, Jesus insists that those who exalt themselves will be humbled and the ones who humble themselves will be exalted.

In contrast to Mark and Matthew, Luke diminishes the faults of the disciples. Instead of showing how they are dispersed at the passion, Luke shows that they have stood by Jesus in his trials. Here Jesus is speaking not just of his passion, but the continual suffering and commitment necessary for service of God's kingdom. Jesus assigns to his disciples the kingdom which his Father had assigned to him. In contrast to Matthew, where the authority to sit on twelve thrones is clearly a future event, Luke shows that Jesus' words refer to the apostolic leadership of the disciples in the early Church. They will share at table with the risen Jesus and they will govern the Church as the twelve patriarchs of the new Israel. In Acts Luke shows how they fulfill their apostolic commission of leadership and service.

Luke 22:31-34

> **Peter's Denial Foretold.** [31]"Simon, Simon, behold Satan has demanded to sift all of you like wheat, [32]but I have prayed that your own faith may not fail; and once you have turned back, you must strengthen your brothers." [33]He said to him, "Lord, I am prepared to go to prison and to die with you." [34]But he replied, "I tell you, Peter, before the cock crows this day, you will deny three times that you know me."

In Jesus' address to Peter, Luke includes verses that have no direct parallels in the other Gospels. Again he brings in the conflict between Satan and Jesus, the apostles, and the Church, which he develops extensively throughout this Gospel and Acts. Satan, who enticed Jesus at the beginning of his ministry, now returns at the end to seduce his disciples (22:3, 31). The vivid simile, "sift like wheat," refers to a violent shaking of faith and a separation from the community, as wheat is separated from chaff.

Jesus' prayer for Peter and his commissioning of him is also unique to Luke. Jesus prays that Peter will remain faithful in trial. "Once you have turned back" implies the failure of Peter, and also his conversion and forgiveness. "You must strengthen your brothers" shows Jesus' solemn commissioning of Peter. While Mark and Matthew record that Jesus himself will gather and lead the scattered flock after his resurrection (Mark 14:27-28; Matt 26:31-32), Luke shows that this task is assigned to Peter. Comparable to Matthew 16:17-19 and John 21:15-17, Peter's weakness is acknowledged, yet he is commissioned by Jesus to be leader and shepherd. Luke anticipates the post-resurrectional prominence of Peter in Acts 1–11.

All the Gospels record Peter's boast that he is willing to die with Jesus. Luke declares that Peter is prepared not just to die with Jesus, but "to go to prison" with him. Three times in Acts, Luke states that Peter was jailed for being a spokesman for Jesus.

Luke 22:35-38

Instructions for the Time of Crisis. [35]He said to them, "When I sent you forth without a money bag or a sack or sandals, were you in need of anything?" "No, nothing," they replied. [36]He said to them, "But now one who has a money bag should take it, and likewise a sack, and one who does not have a sword should sell his cloak and buy one. [37]For I tell you that this scripture must be fulfilled in me, namely, 'He was counted among the wicked'; and indeed what is written about me is coming to fulfillment." [38]Then they said, "Lord, look, there are two swords here." But he replied, "It is enough!"

In his parting instructions to his apostles Jesus speaks of the hostility which they can expect to encounter. On their previous missionary journeys, both in the mission of the Twelve (9:3) and the mission of the seventy-two (10:4), they had been told by Jesus to free themselves from material supports and rely on God's protection. Now, however, they are to prepare themselves well for the persecution they will face in a world hostile to their message.

In referring to the sword, Jesus uses metaphorical language to emphasize the seriousness of their struggle. The sword is used metaphorically in Luke's source to indicate the division that will be created by Jesus' message (Matt 10:34; Luke 12:51). At the arrest of Jesus, when the disciples were ready to use the sword and when one of them struck the servant, Jesus commanded them to stop and he healed the wound inflicted by the sword. It seems evident that the command to bring a sword is symbolically referring to their need to prepare for the coming crisis. However, the disciples misunderstand Jesus' message and produce two swords. Jesus' response, "It is enough," is a rebuke to them and a warning about the temptation to depend on violence.

Luke 22:39-46

The Agony in the Garden. [39]Then going out he went, as was his custom, to the Mount of Olives, and the disciples followed him. [40]When he arrived at the place he said to them, "Pray that you may not undergo the test." [41]After withdrawing about a stone's throw from them and kneeling, he prayed, [42]saying, "Father, if you are willing, take this cup away from me; still, not my will but yours be done." [[43]And to strengthen him an angel from heaven appeared to him. [44]He was in such agony and he prayed so fervently that his sweat became like drops of blood falling on the ground.] [45]When he rose from prayer and returned to his disciples, he found them sleeping from grief. [46]He said to them, "Why are you sleeping? Get up and pray that you may not undergo the test."

While based on Mark's account, the scene in the garden is very differently recounted in Luke's Gospel. The location is given its generic name, Mount of Olives, rather than the more precise Semitic name, Gethsemane. It is noted that it was Jesus' custom to go there, since it was the place of his retirement each night during his Jerusalem ministry. Luke does not focus on the failure of Peter, James, and John to keep watch, but rather on Jesus' withdrawal from all his disciples.

Jesus' exhortation to the disciples, "Pray that you may not undergo the test," occurs at the beginning and end of the scene to form a frame for his own prayer. It is the same prayer taught to them in the Our Father, "do not subject us to the final test" (11:4). His passion will be the test of their fidelity and perseverance. Again the disciples are being tempted by the powers of evil, and Jesus urges them to pray so that the trial will not lead them to apostasy.

The central focus of the scene is the prayer of Jesus. The disposition of Jesus is radically different from Mark's account where Jesus fell to the ground, overcome by grief. Luke omits the strong emotions of distress and sorrow, and says that Jesus knelt down in prayer. His prayer is directed to the will of God, and becomes a model for the prayer of his disciples.

Verses 43 and 44 are probably original, though missing from many ancient manuscripts. They were very likely omitted by later scribes for theological reasons. It was difficult to explain why Jesus would need the help of an angel, and the scene made Jesus sound much too human in the midst of the Arian heresy that attempted to deny Jesus' full divinity. The angel from heaven is an indication that the Father has heard the prayer of Jesus. The angel strengthens him, though the struggle belongs to Jesus himself. The guarding angels are not mentioned in his first struggle with Satan (4:10).

The prayer of Jesus is described as an "agony." In Greek the word refers to the supreme tension of an athlete covered with sweat in victorious combat. Rather than emotional grief, agony connotes the virtues of courage and fortitude. This is the assault the devil threatened to continue while tempting Jesus in the desert (4:13). The sweat of Jesus dramatizes the sense of combat in the scene. "Like drops of blood" is a graphic simile typical of Luke's style, suggesting the intensity of the struggle and anticipating its climax on the cross.

The scene concludes by contrasting the disposition of Jesus and the disciples. Jesus "rose from prayer" while the disciples were "sleeping from grief." Jesus rises because his prayer has made him ready to enter the trial, while the disciples are overcome with fear and distress. Again he admonishes them to pray lest they be assaulted with temptation.

Luke 22:47-53

The Betrayal and Arrest of Jesus. ⁴⁷While he was still speaking, a crowd approached and in front was one of the Twelve, a man named Judas. He went up to Jesus to kiss him. ⁴⁸Jesus said to him, "Judas, are you betraying the Son of Man with a kiss?" ⁴⁹His disciples realized what was about to happen, and they asked, "Lord, shall we strike with a sword?" ⁵⁰And one of them struck the high priest's servant and cut off his right ear. ⁵¹But Jesus said in reply, "Stop, no more of this!" Then he touched the servant's ear and healed him. ⁵²And Jesus said to the chief priests and temple guards and elders who had come for him, "Have you come out as against a robber, with swords and clubs? ⁵³Day after day I was with you in the temple area, and you did not seize me; but this is your hour, the time for the power of darkness."

While Jesus was still urging his disciples to pray, the disciple who did not pray shows the results of his temptation. Though Judas' intention to kiss Jesus is revealed, it does not appear that he did so in Luke. Instead, Jesus addresses Judas by name and interprets his motive as a perversion of the sign of supreme affection into the sign of betrayal. The scene shows that Jesus, not the arresting party, is in control.

Still misunderstanding Jesus' words about how they were to respond to persecution (22:36-38), one of the disciples cut off the right ear of the high priest's servant. Jesus shows his compassion even in the moment of betrayal and arrest by ordering them to stop their violence, as he heals the wounded servant. Thus, Luke foreshows the healing and forgiveness that result from Jesus' saving death.

Luke does not mention the flight of the disciples but places the responsibility for Jesus' arrest on the Jewish religious leaders. Whereas in Mark the arresting party is composed of emissaries of the chief priests, scribes, and elders, Luke says that the chief priests, temple guards, and elders themselves came out against him. The scene ends as Jesus proclaims that it is their hour, the time for the temporary triumph of evil. Luke continues his contrast of light and darkness as an image of the salvation coming to those who are in the darkness of evil and sin (1:79; 11:35).

Luke 22:54-65

Peter's Denial of Jesus. [54]After arresting him they led him away and took him into the house of the high priest; Peter was following at a distance. [55]They lit a fire in the middle of the courtyard and sat around it, and Peter sat down with them. [56]When a maid saw him seated in the light, she looked intently at him and said, "This man too was with him." [57]But he denied it saying, "Woman, I do not know him." [58]A short while later someone else saw him and said, "You too are one of them"; but Peter answered, "My friend, I am not." [59]About an hour later, still another insisted, "Assuredly, this man too was with him, for he also is a Galilean." [60]But Peter said, "My friend, I do not know what you are talking about." Just as he was saying this, the cock crowed, [61]and the Lord turned and looked at Peter; and Peter remembered the word of the Lord, how he had said to him, "Before the cock crows today, you will deny me three times." [62]He went out and began to weep bitterly. [63]The men who held Jesus in custody were ridiculing and beating him. [64]They blindfolded him and questioned him, saying, "Prophesy! Who is it that struck you?" [65]And they reviled him in saying many other things against him.

Following his arrest, Jesus is brought to the house of the high priest. Mark and Matthew narrate the trial of Jesus at this point, while Luke immediately focuses on the denial of Peter and only recounts the trial scene the next morning. This sequence allows Luke to contrast the reaction of Jesus to that of Peter. Jesus submits to arrest because he had prepared in prayer, while Peter fails the temptation because he has not prayed. Satan, who had demanded to sift the disciples like wheat, now tests Peter through the three questions put to him.

The entire scene takes place in the courtyard. Only in Luke does Peter's denial occur in the presence of Jesus. Though Luke diminishes the intensity of Peter's denial and omits his cursing and swearing, the impact of his denial is just as severe. Immediately after the denials, Jesus turns and looks at Peter, creating a more personal realization of his failure. It is this look of Jesus that starts the process of Peter's remorse. It causes Peter to recall not only Jesus' prediction of his denials but also his prayer for Peter and the role that was destined for him (22:32-34).

The mockery of Jesus is also set in the courtyard and before his trial. He is abused as a prophet, a title that Luke has acclaimed for Jesus throughout the Gospel. As Israel had continually rejected and maltreated its prophets (6:23; 11:47; 13:34), now Jesus will die as a prophet in Jerusalem, just as he had predicted (13:33).

Luke 22:66-71

Jesus before the Sanhedrin. ⁶⁶When day came the council of elders of the people met, both chief priests and scribes, and they brought him before their Sanhedrin. ⁶⁷They said, "If you are the Messiah, tell us," but he replied to them, "If I tell you, you will not believe, ⁶⁸and if I question, you will not respond. ⁶⁹But from this time on the Son of Man will be seated at the right hand of the power of God." ⁷⁰They all asked, "Are you then the Son of God?" He replied to them, "You say that I am." ⁷¹Then they said, "What further need have we for testimony? We have heard it from his own mouth."

The interrogation before the Sanhedrin does not seem to be a trial. In contrast to Mark's account, Luke does not mention a night meeting; he says nothing about witnesses; he does not accuse Jesus of seeking to destroy the temple; and there is no formal judgment or condemnation. As in John, Luke describes Jesus' appearance before Pilate as the only trial.

The emphasis in this scene is on Jesus' identity as Messiah, Son of Man, and Son of God. When asked if he is the Messiah, Jesus points to the futility of responding to them. His response is similar to Jeremiah's words when Jeremiah was arrested and stood before Israel's rulers (Jer 38:15).

Jesus then utters a prophecy using the title, Son of Man, the one rejected on earth but vindicated in heaven. Luke changes the time reference in this prophecy, and therefore radically alters Mark's understanding of Jesus' vindication. Mark speaks of the Son of Man enthroned at God's right hand who will come with the clouds at the parousia (Mark 14:62).

By adding "from this time on," Luke makes it clear that Jesus' enthronement in glory is the result of his passion and resurrection. Acts continues to show the prophecy fulfilled as Peter testifies that Jesus is now seated at God's right hand (Acts 2:33), and as the martyr Stephen cries out: "Behold, I see the heavens opened and the Son of Man standing at the right hand of God" (Acts 7:56).

Jesus is the only witness. There is no charge of blasphemy, no guilty verdict, no condemnation to death. But by having the elders speak with one voice, Luke dramatizes Israel's solemn rejection of Jesus as God's prophet.

Luke 23:1-5

Jesus before Pilate. [1]Then the whole assembly of them arose and brought him before Pilate. [2]They brought charges against him, saying, "We found this man misleading our people; he opposes the payment of taxes to Caesar and maintains that he is the Messiah, a king." [3]Pilate asked him, "Are you the king of the Jews?" He said to him in reply, "You say so." [4]Pilate then addressed the chief priests and the crowds, 'I find this man not guilty." [5]But they were adamant and said, "He is inciting the people with his teaching throughout all Judea, from Galilee where he began even to here."

Luke expands the narrative of the trial by carefully laying out three charges leveled against Jesus. "Misleading our people" is a generic accusation referring to Jesus' teachings. The second charge, opposing the payment of taxes to Caesar, is clearly false since Jesus had openly endorsed paying to Caesar what was Caesar's (20:25). The third charge recalls the proclamation of Jesus as king during his triumphal entry into Jerusalem (19:38).

Pilate's personal inquiry is reduced to one question: "Are you the king of the Jews?" Jesus gives the same ambiguous response found in all the Gospels. Then Pilate dismisses the charges, finding Jesus "not guilty." This is the first of three declarations of Jesus' innocence by Pilate.

Luke 23:6-12

Jesus before Herod. [6]On hearing this Pilate asked if the man was a Galilean; [7]and upon learning that he was under Herod's juris-

diction, he sent him to Herod who was in Jerusalem at that time.
⁸Herod was very glad to see Jesus; he had been wanting to see him
for a long time, for he had heard about him and had been hoping
to see him perform some sign. ⁹He questioned him at length, but
he gave him no answer. ¹⁰The chief priests and scribes, meanwhile,
stood by accusing him harshly. ¹¹[Even] Herod and his soldiers
treated him contemptuously and mocked him, and after clothing
him in resplendent garb, he sent him back to Pilate. ¹²Herod and
Pilate became friends that very day, even though they had been
enemies formerly.

The mention of Galilee gives Pilate the opportunity to divert the
trial to King Herod, Tetrarch of Galilee. Herod played an important
role throughout Luke's Gospel. Jesus was born during the reign of
Herod's father, Herod the Great (1:5). The word of God came to John
the Baptist while Herod was Tetrarch of Galilee (3:1), and this same
Herod threw him into prison (3:19). As noted in the trial scene, Herod
had wanted to see Jesus after hearing about his reputation (9:9), and
later Jesus was told that Herod sought to kill him (13:31).

The trial before Herod is recounted only in Luke. By adding this
trial to the passion account, Luke adds another witness in defense of
Jesus. Both a king and a governor now agree on Jesus' innocence. Luke
shows a similar agreement in Paul's trial in Acts. After first being tried
by the Sanhedrin (Acts 22:30f), Paul was tried by the procurator who
then referred the case to King Agrippa who was in Caesarea for a visit
(Acts 25). In both trials the Roman governor and a visiting king attest
to the innocence of the accused.

The supreme irony of the scene is expressed in the reconciliation
of Herod and Pilate who had previously been enemies. They were un-
able to free Jesus who stood innocent before them. Though Jesus was
humiliated by these representatives of worldly power, in his suffering
he joined them together in friendship.

Just as Jesus was led before Herod and Pilate, he told his followers,
"They will hand you over to kings and governors because of my name"
(21:12). In Acts, Luke again explains how Herod and Pontius Pilate
gathered against Jesus as the community prayed for courage in their
trials. Throughout Acts, Luke shows the parallel treatment of Jesus and
his Church, and holds Jesus as the model for proper behavior in the
midst of persecution.

Luke 23:13-25

¹³Pilate then summoned the chief priests, the rulers, and the people ¹⁴and said to them, "You brought this man to me and accused him of inciting the people to revolt. I have conducted my investigation in your presence and have not found this man guilty of the charges you have brought against him, ¹⁵nor did Herod, for he sent him back to us. So no capital crime has been committed by him. ¹⁶Therefore I shall have him flogged and then release him."[¹⁷] **The Sentence of Death.** ¹⁸But all together they shouted out, "Away with this man! Release Barabbas to us." ¹⁹(Now Barabbas had been imprisoned for a rebellion that had taken place in the city and for murder.) ²⁰Again Pilate addressed them, still wishing to release Jesus, ²¹but they continued their shouting, "Crucify him! Crucify him!" ²²Pilate addressed them a third time, "What evil has this man done? I found him guilty of no capital crime. Therefore I shall have him flogged and then release him." ²³With loud shouts, however, they persisted in calling for his crucifixion, and their voices prevailed. ²⁴The verdict of Pilate was that their demand should be granted. ²⁵So he released the man who had been imprisoned for rebellion and murder, for whom they asked, and he handed Jesus over to them to deal with as they wished.

Pilate gathers a representative assembly of Israel and summarizes the juridical proceedings: the arrest, the accusations, the investigation, Pilate's verdict supported by that of Herod, and the acquittal. Assuring the crowd of the legality of the proceedings, Pilate solemnly declares that Jesus has done nothing to deserve death. He determines to discipline Jesus, Luke's only hint of the brutal scourging, and then release him.

Pilate's decision to release Jesus turns the crowd into a shouting mob. They call for the release of Barabbas and for the crucifixion of Jesus. Pilate continues to defend Jesus and declares his innocence for the third time. Yet Pilate is not strong enough and the crowd's persistence causes him to yield to their demands.

Luke's account of the Barabbas incident is the shortest of the Gospels. Verse 17 is not found in most ancient manuscripts, and is generally regarded as a gloss from Mark 15:6. It was added later to explain the custom of releasing a prisoner at Passover. Luke notes twice that the crimes of Barabbas were rebellion and murder. The trial of Jesus becomes the trial of Israel as they clearly reject Jesus and choose murderous rebellion. Luke reemphasizes that choice in Acts 3:14: "You denied the Holy and Righteous One and asked that a murderer be released to you." Pilate never condemns Jesus to die, but hands him over to them "to deal with as they wished."

Luke 23:26-32

The Way of the Cross. [26]As they led him away they took hold of a certain Simon, a Cyrenian, who was coming in from the country; and after laying the cross on him, they made him carry it behind Jesus. [27]A large crowd of people followed Jesus, including many women who mourned and lamented him. [28]Jesus turned to them and said, "Daughters of Jerusalem, do not weep for me; weep instead for yourselves and for your children, [29]for indeed, the days are coming when people will say, 'Blessed are the barren, the wombs that never bore and the breasts that never nursed.' [30]At that time people will say to the mountains, 'Fall upon us!' and to the hills, 'Cover us!' [31]for if these things are done when the wood is green what will happen when it is dry?" [32]Now two others, both criminals, were led away with him to be executed.

Luke continues the passion narrative with an extended explanation of events on the way to Golgotha. We can presume that Jesus was breaking down under the weight of the cross, so Simon was forced to help him carry it. Luke's hand is evident here as he adds "behind Jesus." Simon, then, becomes an image of discipleship as he takes up the cross and follows Jesus (9:23; 14:27).

The women of Jerusalem consoled prisoners who were condemned to die. In Luke, the women represent the people of Jerusalem and become the recipients of Jesus' final prophecy of the city's destruction. Jesus wept over Jerusalem when he first entered it, and now as he finally leaves it he tells the women to weep for the city. Jeremiah had exhorted the women of Jerusalem to such weeping as God speaks about judgment on Jerusalem (Jer 9:16-20).

Throughout Luke's Gospel "the coming days" refer to the destruction of Jerusalem. As Jesus entered Jerusalem, he spoke of its coming destruction "because you did not recognize the time of your visitation" (19:44). In Luke 21, Jesus speaks of Jerusalem surrounded by armies (v. 20) and trampled underfoot by the Gentiles (v. 24), "for these days are the time of punishment" (v. 22). In his final oracle, Jesus prophesies the fate that awaits the inhabitants of Jerusalem because of their rejection of him.

The harsh prophecy echoes the words of Hosea 10:8. In this passage the people of Samaria ask the mountains and hills to protect them. They seek to hide from God's wrath and escape punishment for their deeds.

The prophecy is continued by citing what must have been a common proverb. Its exact meaning is uncertain, though Jesus seems to be comparing his own passion to green wood, difficult to kindle, and the suffering of Jerusalem to dry wood, easy to kindle and to be consumed in fire. If Jesus who is innocent has experienced so much suffering, how much suffering awaits the guilty Jerusalem?

Finally, Luke notes that two others were led away with Jesus for execution. Luke uses the word which means "criminals," rather than the more specific "robbers" or "revolutionaries" found in Mark and Matthew. Thus the prophecy recalled in 22:37 is fulfilled, "He was counted among the wicked."

Luke 23:33-43

The Crucifixion. ³³When they came to the place called the Skull, they crucified him and the criminals there, one on his right, the other on his left. ³⁴[Then Jesus said, "Father, forgive them, they know not what they do."] They divided his garments by casting lots. ³⁵The people stood by and watched; the rulers, meanwhile, sneered at him and said, "He saved others, let him save himself if he is the chosen one, the Messiah of God." ³⁶Even the soldiers jeered at him. As they approached to offer him wine ³⁷they called out, "If you are King of the Jews, save yourself." ³⁸Above him there was an inscription that read, "This is the King of the Jews."

³⁹Now one of the criminals hanging there reviled Jesus, saying, "Are you not the Messiah? Save yourself and us." ⁴⁰The other, however, rebuking him, said in reply, "Have you no fear of God, for you are subject to the same condemnation? ⁴¹And indeed, we have been condemned justly, for the sentence we received corresponds to our crimes, but this man has done nothing criminal." ⁴²Then he said, "Jesus, remember me when you come into your kingdom." ⁴³He replied to him, "Amen, I say to you, today you will be with me in Paradise."

Though verse 34 is missing from many ancient manuscripts, Jesus' forgiveness of his executioners is totally consistent with Luke's writing. Stephen utters similar words when being executed by the Jews of

Jerusalem (Acts 7:60). If the verse is original, it was probably dropped at a later period when the Christian community was undergoing persecution from the Jews.

Luke's Gospel retains a favorable judgment of the people of Israel. In contrast to Mark and Matthew he distinguishes between the people and their leaders. In Luke's account the people do not revile Jesus and shake their heads, nor do they chide him about rebuilding the temple or coming down from the cross. Instead, the people stand by while their rulers taunt Jesus, and they will return home "beating their breasts" (23:48).

Jesus is ridiculed by three very different strata of society: the rulers, the soldiers, and a criminal. The group is inclusive, with both Jewish leaders and Gentile soldiers joining in the mockery. The content of each mockery is the same: though Jesus claims to be the Messiah, he cannot save himself. They ridicule both his identity and his mission.

The scene of derision is followed by a scene of acceptance. The contrast between the two criminals on his right and his left is strong and dramatic, representing the conflicting judgments that people will continue to have about Jesus. Luke alone recounts the dialogue of Jesus with the repentant criminal. While pointing again to Jesus' innocence, Luke shows his saving mercy in this climactic scene. Unlike those who taunt Jesus, the criminal recognizes Jesus' kingship and asks for a share in his kingdom. Jesus promises the criminal that he will share in his victory, thus stressing the saving effects of Jesus' death.

Luke 23:44-49

> **The Death of Jesus.** 44It was now about noon and darkness came over the whole land until three in the afternoon 45because of an eclipse of the sun. Then the veil of the temple was torn down the middle. 46Jesus cried out in a loud voice, "Father, into your hands I commend my spirit"; and when he had said this he breathed his last. 47The centurion who witnessed what had happened glorified God and said, "This man was innocent beyond doubt." 48When all the people who had gathered for this spectacle saw what had happened, they returned home beating their breasts; 49but all his acquaintances stood at a distance, including the women who had followed him from Galilee and saw these events.

Luke's account of Jesus' death differs significantly from Mark's. He includes an explanation of the darkness and immediately follows with the notice concerning the temple veil. Jesus does not cry out in abandonment with the words of Psalm 22; rather, he dies with the peaceful words of Psalm 31. The centurion does not proclaim Jesus as Son of God, but testifies to his innocence. Luke also modifies the reactions of the crowd and Jesus' followers as the scene ends.

The darkness and the rending of the temple veil add a cosmic and apocalyptic dimension to the death of Jesus. This scene is related to Jesus' premonition concerning evil's "hour" and the "power of darkness" (22:53). Luke explains the darkness by saying that the sunlight had failed. This does not necessarily imply an eclipse of the sun, but could be the dust-laden sirocco wind or any phenomena that impede the sun's brightness. The darkness provides an ominous background for Jesus' death. Luke also places the rending of the temple veil before the death of Jesus to join it with the cataclysmic darkness. Luke probably intends that the rending represent the new access to God's presence for all people, Jews and Gentiles alike, because of Jesus' death.

Luke does not record Jesus' cry of abandonment from Psalm 22. His Gentile readers would not have known that the psalm concludes with confident trust in God; rather, they would have interpreted the words as a cry of despair. Instead, Luke indicates that Jesus dies with the peaceful words of Psalm 31:6, "Into your hands I commend my spirit." Jesus addresses these words to his Father, emphasizing his filial relationship to God, so prominent in Luke. Throughout the Gospel Jesus is depicted as being handed over into the hands of men. Now at his death he entrusts himself into the hands of the Father. Stephen, at his death, utters similar words of resignation, though addressed to Jesus (Acts 7:59).

The words of the centurion seem much weaker in Luke's account than the confident profession of faith recorded in Mark and Matthew. On one level, the Gentile centurion is proclaiming that Jesus is innocent; however, Luke probably intends the words to mean more. The words can also mean "righteous," and Luke will later refer to Jesus by the messianic title, Righteous One (Acts 3:14; 7:52; 22:14).

The conclusion of the scene is reformulated by Luke to give emphasis to those who witness these events. The people "contemplated" what had happened and went home beating their breasts, a sign of grief and contrition. Luke shows the salvific quality of Jesus' death, as the crowd already is moved to repent. He also notes the presence of Jesus' acquaintances who stood at a distance. Since Luke portrays the disciples far less harshly than Mark, he does not report their desertion when Jesus was arrested. The mention of his acquaintances here must refer to at least some of his disciples. Finally, the women from Galilee, distinguished from the daughters of Jerusalem, are mentioned as witnesses to Jesus' death, since they will also be witnesses of his resurrection.

Luke 23:50-56

The Burial of Jesus. [50]Now there was a virtuous and righteous man named Joseph who, though he was a member of the council, [51]had not consented to their plan of action. He came from the Jewish town of Arimathea and was awaiting the kingdom of God. [52]He went to Pilate and asked for the body of Jesus. [53]After he had taken the body down, he wrapped it in a linen cloth and laid him in a rock-hewn tomb in which no one had yet been buried. [54]It was the day of preparation, and the sabbath was about to begin. [55]The women who had come from Galilee with him followed behind, and when they had seen the tomb and the way in which his body was laid in it, [56]they returned and prepared spices and perfumed oils. Then they rested on the sabbath according to the commandment.

The passion account ends with the burial of Jesus by Joseph, a Jew from Arimathea. Luke makes it clear that, though Joseph was a member of the Sanhedrin, he had not agreed to Jesus' death. Luke shows in Acts that many Jewish leaders are sympathetic to the followers of Jesus and even join the faith (Acts 5:34-39; 6:7). Joseph is described in the same way as Zechariah, Elizabeth, Simeon, and Anna in the infancy narratives. He is "righteous" and "awaiting the kingdom of God." Thus he is placed in that long line of faithful Israelites awaiting God's redemption.

Luke omits many of the details of the burial scene that Mark's narrative includes, such as Joseph's courage, Pilate's assurance that Jesus had died, the stone rolled across the tomb, and the naming of the women. Luke adds a significant element to Mark's narrative by noting that Joseph laid Jesus in a tomb "in which no one had yet been buried." Just as Jesus rode into Jerusalem on a colt "on which no one had ever sat," signifying the uniqueness of that event, his death and burial was also inimitable.

Luke is careful to point out the obedience to the Sabbath law. Since it was nearing sundown and the Sabbath was about to begin, the women from Galilee took careful note of the tomb and Jesus' burial so they could return after the Sabbath to anoint his body according to the Jewish custom. When they returned home they prepared the spices and perfumed oil in advance so they could observe the proper Sabbath rest.

The burial scene forms a transition from the passion account to the resurrection. Both Joseph's burial of Jesus and the women's witness of the tomb establish that Jesus had indeed died and was buried in a unique tomb remembered by them all. The final note concerning the Sabbath rest forms a temporal transition leading to the morning of resurrection.

Luke 24:1-12

The Resurrection of Jesus. ¹But at daybreak on the first day of the week they took the spices they had prepared and went to the tomb. ²They found the stone rolled away from the tomb; ³but when they entered, they did not find the body of the Lord Jesus. ⁴While they were puzzling over this, behold, two men in dazzling garments appeared to them. ⁵They were terrified and bowed their faces to the ground. They said to them, "Why do you seek the living one among the dead? ⁶He is not here, but he has been raised. Remember what he said to you while he was still in Galilee, ⁷that the Son of Man must be handed over to sinners and be crucified, and rise on the third day." ⁸And they remembered his words. ⁹Then they returned from the tomb and announced all these things to the eleven and to all the others. ¹⁰The women were Mary Magdalene, Joanna, and Mary the mother of James; the others who accompanied them also told this to the apostles, ¹¹but their story seemed like nonsense and they did not believe them. ¹²But Peter got up and ran to the tomb, bent down, and saw the burial cloths alone; then he went home amazed at what had happened.

The principal source for Luke's description of the women's visit to the tomb is Mark 16:1-8. However, Luke's account has its own distinctive characteristics. Many of the changes and additions show how the events of the resurrection culminate Luke's total plan for the Gospel. The visit to the tomb and the resurrection appearances also form a transition to Luke's second volume, the Acts of the Apostles.

All the evangelists set the discovery of the empty tomb on the first day of the week. This is the day, as Luke will show in Acts 20:7, the Christians gathered for the breaking of the bread. Luke recounts all from Galilee took careful note of the tomb and Jesus' burial so they could return after the Sabbath to anoint his body according to the Jewish custom. When they returned home they prepared the spices and perfumed oil in advance so they could observe the proper Sabbath rest.

The burial scene forms a transition from the passion account to the resurrection. Both Joseph's burial of Jesus and the women's witness of the tomb establish that Jesus had indeed died and was buried in a unique tomb remembered by them all. The final note concerning the Sabbath rest forms a temporal transition leading to the morning of resurrection.

Luke 24:1-12

The Resurrection of Jesus. ¹But at daybreak on the first day of the week they took the spices they had prepared and went to the tomb. ²They found the stone rolled away from the tomb; ³but when they entered, they did not find the body of the Lord Jesus. ⁴While they were puzzling over this, behold, two men in dazzling garments appeared to them. ⁵They were terrified and bowed their faces to the ground. They said to them, "Why do you seek the living one among the dead? ⁶He is not here, but he has been raised. Remember what he said to you while he was still in Galilee, ⁷that the Son of Man must be handed over to sinners and be crucified, and rise on the third day." ⁸And they remembered his words. ⁹Then they returned from the tomb and announced all these things to the eleven and to all the others. ¹⁰The women were Mary Magdalene, Joanna, and Mary the mother of James; the others who accompanied them also told this to the apostles, ¹¹but their story seemed like nonsense and they did not believe them. ¹²But Peter got up and ran to the tomb, bent down, and saw the burial cloths alone; then he went home amazed at what had happened.

The principal source for Luke's description of the women's visit to the tomb is Mark 16:1-8. However, Luke's account has its own distinctive characteristics. Many of the changes and additions show how the events of the resurrection culminate Luke's total plan for the Gospel. The visit to the tomb and the resurrection appearances also form a transition to Luke's second volume, the Acts of the Apostles.

All the evangelists set the discovery of the empty tomb on the first day of the week. This is the day, as Luke will show in Acts 20:7, the Christians gathered for the breaking of the bread. Luke recounts all the events of this final chapter as happening on this same day. This is the first day of a new age, the day Christians will set apart each week as the day of resurrection.

Luke notes that the two men who announced the resurrection wore dazzling garments suggestive of their other worldly nature. Later in the account they are said to be angels (24:23). Throughout the Gospel, those who proclaim the message of Jesus or perform some divinely appointed task are paired. The seventy-two are sent out in pairs. Likewise, two men prepared for Jesus' entry into Jerusalem and for the Passover meal. Two appeared with Jesus in the transfiguration, two will encounter him on the road to Emmaus, and two will also interpret the ascension of Jesus (Acts 1:10).

The two men begin by challenging the women's focus on the tomb: "Why do you seek the living one among the dead?" This is similar to the challenge given by the two men in white garments at the ascension of Jesus: "Why are you standing there looking at the sky?" (Acts 1:11) After each challenging question the proclamation is given that sets the hearers off on their mission.

Unlike Mark and Matthew, Luke says nothing of resurrection appearances in Galilee. Instead, Jerusalem remains the focal point within Luke's writings. It is the place toward which the Gospel proceeds, the city of Jesus' destiny, and the place from which the ministry of the early Church disseminates. Rather than telling the disciples that Jesus is going before them to Galilee (Mark 16:7; Matt 28:7), the messengers ask the women to remember what he had said to them while he was still in Galilee. Luke must have known about appearances of Jesus in other areas, but in the interest of his overall literary plan, he ends his Gospel only with events in Jerusalem.

The names of the women vary slightly in the resurrection narratives of each Gospel. Mary Magdalene is common to all four Gospels and is named first in each. Joanna is known only from Luke and is earlier described as the wife of Herod's steward (8:3). Though the women proclaimed the message to the Eleven, it did not move them to faith. Luke makes it clear that the apostles did not accept the women's report since it seemed like nonsense. It will be only an actual experience of the risen Lord that will bring them to faith.

In verse 12 Luke seems to be drawing on a tradition that told of the visit of Peter to the empty tomb, in addition to the visit by the women. John drew on the same tradition in his account which has many similarities (John 20:2-10). Peter's experience leads only to amazement and not belief, for he has experienced only the empty tomb and not yet the risen Christ.

Luke 24:13-35

The Appearance on the Road to Emmaus. [13]Now that very day two of them were going to a village seven miles from Jerusalem called Emmaus, [14]and they were conversing about all the things that had occurred. [15]And it happened that while they were conversing and debating, Jesus himself drew near and walked with them, [16]but their eyes were prevented from recognizing him. [17]He asked them, "What are you discussing as you walk along?" They stopped, looking downcast. [18]One of them, named Cleopas, said to him in reply, "Are you the only visitor to Jerusalem who does not know of the things that have taken place there in these days?" [19]And he replied to them, "What sort of things?" They said to him, "The things that happened to Jesus the Nazarene, who was a prophet mighty in deed and word before God and all the people, [20]how our chief priests and rulers both handed him over to a sentence of death and crucified him. [21]But we were hoping that he would be the one to redeem Israel; and besides all this, it is now the third day since this took place. [22]Some women from our group, however, have astounded us: they were at the tomb early in the morning [23]and did not find his body; they came back and reported that they had indeed seen a vision of angels who announced that he was alive. [24]Then some of those with us went to the tomb and found things just as the women had described, but him they did not see." [25]And he said to them, "Oh, how foolish you are! How slow of heart to believe all that the prophets spoke! [26]Was it not necessary that the Messiah should suffer these things and enter into his glory?" [27]Then beginning with Moses and all the prophets, he interpreted to them what referred to him in all the scriptures. [28]As they approached the village to which they were going, he gave the impression that he was going on farther. [29]But they urged him, "Stay with us, for it is nearly evening and the day is almost over." So he went in to stay with them. [30]And it happened that, while he was with them at table, he took bread, said the blessing, broke it, and gave it to them. [31]With that their eyes were opened and they recognized him, but he vanished from their sight. [32]Then they said to each other, "Were not our hearts burning [within us] while he spoke to us on the way and opened the scriptures to us?" [33]So they set out at once and returned to Jerusalem where they found

gathered together the eleven and those with them [34]who were saying, "The Lord has truly been raised and has appeared to Simon!"
[35]Then the two recounted what had taken place on the way and
how he was made known to them in the breaking of the bread.

Following the account of the visit to the empty tomb, each Gospel
writer goes his own way in the resurrection narrative. In Luke, Jesus
appears the same day, the first day of the week, and is seen by two
of the disciples who had been with the Eleven earlier in the day to hear
the report of the women (24:9). Of the two disciples, only Cleopas is
identified. The anonymity of the other and the fact that Cleopas is mentioned only here indicate that the two represent all followers of Jesus.

These two disciples were returning to their home near Jerusalem
after celebrating the feast of Passover in the city. The location of Emmaus has been much debated and there is no possibility of being certain about the site of the village. Luke says it is sixty stadia from
Jerusalem, or about seven miles. It is only important for Luke's Gospel
that it be within the vicinity of Jerusalem.

This resurrection appearance has several parallels to another Lucan
account, the meeting of Philip with the Ethiopian eunuch (Acts 8:26-40).
In both accounts the one traveling on a journey meets a stranger who
interprets the Scriptures to show that the Messiah must suffer. In each
a sacramental action is followed by a sudden disappearance.

As the two travelers are conversing on their way to Emmaus, Jesus
overtakes them from the rear. Thinking him to be another pilgrim
returning home, the disciples do not recognize him. Though they see
him physically, the point of the description is to show that they are
spiritually blind because they do not understand. This theme of recognition frames the entire account as the disciples move from not knowing Jesus to recognition of him following the conversation.

Jesus introduces the dialogue by inquiring into the subject of the
disciples' conversation and asking to be told about the recent events.
They describe Jesus as a great prophet and speak about their unful-
filled hopes that he was the messianic deliverer who would set Israel
free from Roman occupation. Recounting Jesus' crucifixion and death
and the discovery of the empty tomb by the women that morning, the
disciples remained skeptical because they did not see him.

When Jesus responds, he corrects their impression of him. He shows
them that the Messiah had to suffer by his insisting on "all" that the
prophets spoke. Jesus gives no specific references here, but shows how

the writings of Moses and the prophets prepare for the Gospel and are fulfilled in Jesus.

Jesus shows that because the Messiah has suffered, he is now in his glory. Glory is the splendor associated with the presence of God. Jesus has already entered into the glory of the Father, and it is from this state of glory that he appears to the disciples.

The disciples offer hospitality and urge Jesus to stay with them. The request connotes their need for the deeper, abiding presence of the Lord. The indication that it was evening and the day was almost over alludes to the contrast of light and darkness. Sundown was also when the Christians gathered for their assembly and the breaking of the bread.

When they recline at table, Jesus assumes the role of the host. His gestures over the bread recall the Last Supper and become Luke's way of describing the Eucharist in Acts. As Jesus blesses and breaks the bread the disciples recognize him. "Their eyes were opened" means they were able to see him with the eyes of faith because of their deeper understanding.

As the narrative reaches its climax in the disciples' recognition of their guest, Jesus vanishes from their sight. They now realize how the risen Lord will be present to the assembled disciples. They remember that their hearts were burning as Jesus was explaining the Scriptures to them. They know that it was his risen presence they were experiencing all along. It was only after understanding the Scriptures that they were prepared to recognize Jesus in the breaking of the bread. Thus the account reflects the twofold structure of the Christian assembly for the breaking of the bread and the dynamic relationship between word and sacrament. Both the interpretation of the Scriptures and the breaking of the bread are actions of the risen Christ in which his presence is made real for the Church.

Luke 24:36-49

The Appearance to the Disciples in Jerusalem. [36]While they were still speaking about this, he stood in their midst and said to them, "Peace be with you." [37]But they were startled and terrified and thought that they were seeing a ghost. [38]Then he said to them, "Why are you troubled? And why do questions arise in your hearts? [39]Look at my hands and my feet, that it is I myself. Touch me and see, because a ghost does not have flesh and bones as you can see I have." [40]And as he said this, he showed them his hands and his feet. [41]While they were still incredulous for joy and were amazed, he asked them, "Have you anything here to eat?" [42]They gave him a piece of baked fish; [43]he took it and ate it in front of them.

[44]He said to them, "These are my words that I spoke to you while I was still with you, that everything written about me in the law of Moses and in the prophets and psalms must be fulfilled." [45]Then he opened their minds to understand the scriptures. [46]And he said to them, "Thus it is written that the Messiah would suffer and rise from the dead on the third day [47]and that repentance, for the forgiveness of sins, would be preached in his name to all the nations, beginning from Jerusalem. [48]You are witnesses of these things. [49]And [behold] I am sending the promise of my Father upon you; but stay in the city until you are clothed with power from on high."

This resurrection appearance is experienced by the Eleven and those gathered with them in Jerusalem immediately after the two disciples return from Emmaus with their report. It parallels the Emmaus account in several ways. In both scenes Jesus' presence is not understood, an instruction from the Scriptures leads to understanding, a meal is shared, and Jesus departs. While the presence of Jesus in word and sacrament is emphasized in the Emmaus account, his bodily presence and the disciples' mission is central here.

Again we find similarities in Luke and John that indicate a tradition used by both. In John, as in Luke, Jesus stands in the midst of his disciples and says, "Peace be with you." He shows them the wounds of his passion and the disciples respond with joy. Jesus commissions his disciples and assures them of the presence of his Spirit (John 20:19-22).

The appearance of the risen Jesus provokes a variety of reactions by his disciples: they are startled, terrified, troubled, incredulous, joyful and amazed. Jesus stands among them with his message of "peace." The greeting of peace wishes for the receiver a completeness and fulfillment that is not possible from the world but is brought by Christ's victory (1:79; 2:14; 19:42).

The passage tells us that the risen presence of Jesus is a bodily presence. In contrast to those who would interpret the resurrection as simply a return to spiritual existence, Luke insists on the bodily reality. The disciples touch him, he shows them his hands and his feet, and he eats with them. Jesus points out that a spirit does not have flesh and bones as he has. He establishes his identity and convinces them that he is the same person who lived among them before his death.

The disciples listen intently as Jesus explains what pertains to him from the Scriptures. The law, the prophets, and the psalms is a traditional way of referring to the entire Old Testament. Only in light of the resurrection can it be seen how God's salvific plan is fulfilled in Jesus. This becomes the basis of the apostles' preaching shown to us throughout Acts. The core of their preaching would be the passion and resurrection of the Messiah and the necessity of repentance for the forgiveness of sins.

As in the finale of Matthew's Gospel, Jesus commissions his followers to carry out a future mission in his name. Luke introduces here the important role the disciples are to play in the new phase of salvation history: they are to be witnesses, beginning in Jerusalem and extending to all the nations. The goal of Jesus' journey, Jerusalem, now becomes the starting point from which the message of salvation will extend to the ends of the earth (Acts 1:8).

The disciples are told to wait in Jerusalem until they are invested with "power from on high." Commissioned by Jesus, they will also be given the power needed to carry it out through the Spirit. "The Spirit from on high" was foretold by Isaiah for the messianic times (Isa 32:15; Wis 9:17), and it is this "power" that had filled Jesus (4:14; 5:17; 6:19). The command to wait in Jerusalem for the coming of the Spirit provides the transition to the Acts of the Apostles.

Luke 24:50-53

The Ascension. 50Then he led them [out] as far as Bethany, raised his hands, and blessed them. 51As he blessed them he parted from them and was taken up to heaven. 52They did him homage and then returned to Jerusalem with great joy, 53and they were continually in the temple praising God.

Luke is unique in speaking of Jesus' departure at the end of his appearances. It brings to a close his account of Jesus' life. The ascension will also begin his account of the early Church in Acts.

The ascension is the end of Jesus' exodus (9:31) which Luke develops throughout the Gospel. In 9:51 Luke begins the narration of the journey to Jerusalem, "when the days for his being taken up were fulfilled." His passage to the Father through death and resurrection was completed in his ascension.

In the Gospel, the ascension occurs on the same day as the resurrection, whereas in Acts 1:9-11, it took place forty days later. The essential affirmation of both accounts is that Jesus is with the Father in glory. The Gospel account shows the necessary unity of the resurrection and ascension as the glorification of Jesus. In Acts the ascension is the prelude for a new phase of salvation history, the era of the Church. The number forty marks a period of transition in the Scriptures: forty years in the desert are Israel's passage from slavery to freedom; forty days in the desert prepare for Jesus' public life; forty days of resurrection appearances form the transition to the new age of the Church.

As Jesus' final action, he "raised his hands and blessed them." This is the priestly blessing over the people as given by Aaron and the priests of Israel after him (Lev 9:22; Sir 50:20). As Jesus blesses his disciples, they bow down in adoration since the resurrection has revealed his divinity.

The Gospel ends where it began, in the temple of Jerusalem. The followers of Jesus were joyful and continually praised God in the temple. In this way Luke begins his description of the community life of the Church and prepares for the Acts of the Apostles (Acts 2:46; 3:1; 5:42).

The Passion and Resurrection According to John

The Gospel of John is dramatically different in character from the other three Gospels. It grew out of a different community which reflected on the events of Jesus' life in a unique way. Throughout the Gospel the incidents received from the tradition are given a fuller meaning as they become symbols that reveal more fully the mystery of Christ and invite the reader to deeper faith. These "signs" performed by Jesus throughout the Gospel find their fulfillment in the passion and resurrection. The crucified-glorified One is the light of the world, the true bread from heaven, the Good Shepherd, the way, the truth, and the life.

The whole Gospel is a progressive revelation of the glory of God's only Son. From his pre-existence with the Father, he comes to reveal the Father and then to return to the Father. The high point of Jesus' mission is the "hour" of his glorification when he passes to his Father through death and resurrection. In this hour he reveals himself and communicates the life of God to those who accept him and commit themselves to him.

John's passion account is permeated with the glory of the resurrection. Suffering and evil have no real power over him. It is the sovereign Son of God who freely chooses to lay down his life because of his utter certitude that he will take it up again. He does not pray to be delivered from his hour, but confidently realizes that it is the goal of his life.

The accounts of John radiate the divine majesty of Jesus. Truly, to have seen him is to have seen the Father. The Romans and the Jews fall to the ground before the divine name, "I AM." Jesus reigns victoriously from the cross as his kingship is universally proclaimed. Thomas expresses the essence of faith as he proclaims, "My Lord and my God."

As Jesus is glorified in his death and resurrection, he hands over his Spirit. The life-giving Spirit is the outcome of his saving work, and forms the community of his Church. From the cross Jesus creates the family of disciples, and as his life is fulfilled, he dispenses the sources of eternal life from his wounded side. In his risen presence Jesus continues to show himself to his followers and sends them into the world so that all may have life in his name.

John 18:1-11

Jesus Arrested. [1]When he had said this, Jesus went out with his disciples across the Kidron valley to where there was a garden, into which he and his disciples entered. [2]Judas his betrayer also knew the place, because Jesus had often met there with his disciples. [3]So Judas got a band of soldiers and guards from the chief priests and the Pharisees and went there with lanterns, torches, and weapons. [4]Jesus, knowing everything that was going to happen to him, went out and said to them, "Whom are you looking for?" [5]They answered him, "Jesus the Nazorean." He said to them, "I AM." Judas his betrayer was also with them. [6]When he said to them, "I AM," they turned away and fell to the ground. [7]So he again asked them, "Whom are you looking for?" They said, "Jesus the Nazorean." [8]Jesus answered, "I told you that I AM. So if you are looking for me, let these men go." [9]This was to fulfill what he had said, "I have not lost any of those you gave me." [10]Then Simon Peter, who had a sword, drew it, struck the high priest's slave, and cut off his right ear. The slave's name was Malchus. [11]Jesus said to Peter, "Put your sword into its scabbard. Shall I not drink the cup that the Father gave me?"

John's passion account begins with the arrest of Jesus in the garden. After the Last Discourse (14–17), which is very unlike the other Gospels, John returns to the narrative events of the passion. He describes the incidents of Jesus' "hour," when Jesus will show his love for his own to the end (13:1). Jesus is totally in control of what is happening as his triumphant resurrection already penetrates the scenes of the passion.

Unlike the other evangelists, John does not portray Jesus praying in Gethsemane for deliverance from his impending suffering. However, elements of Jesus' prayer in the garden are present elsewhere. In 12:27 Jesus speaks of his troubled spirit; yet with divine resolve, he calls upon the Father to fulfill the process of his glorification. John differs from the other Gospel writers by introducing Roman soldiers into the garden scene. The presence of a Roman cohort and the tribune (18:12) shows Roman collusion in the action against Jesus. It prepares us for the dramatic confrontation of Jesus and Pilate, central to John's passion account, and it reflects the opposition between Rome and Christianity at the time of John's writing.

When Judas was last presented, he had gone off into the night (13:30). It is in this dark night that people stumble because they do not have the light (11:10; 12:35). John alone mentions that the arresting party brings lanterns and torches. Because they did not accept the true light of the world, the ministers of darkness need lamps. The drama of the passion will be played out within this contrast of light and darkness.

Fully aware of everything that was going to happen to him, Jesus takes the initiative and dominates the scene. Judas does not give Jesus the fateful kiss as in the other Gospels. Rather, Jesus goes forth to meet Judas and the arresting party. On one level, Jesus' response, "I AM," serves to identify Jesus, as the kiss of Judas had identified Jesus in the other Gospels. Yet in John, "I AM" expresses Jesus' divinity (4:26; 6:20; 8:24, 28, 58; 13:19). It is the divine name revealed to Moses in Exodus 3:14. Before the divine presence of Jesus, they all turned away and fell to the ground.

Though all four Gospels describe the violent slashing of the servant's ear, only John identifies by name those involved. Peter, lacking in his understanding of Jesus' destiny, tries to prevent his arrest through the human power of violence. Malchus, the high priest's slave, is mentioned only in this passage.

John 18:12-14

¹²So the band of soldiers, the tribune, and the Jewish guards seized Jesus, bound him, ¹³and brought him to Annas first. He was the father-in-law of Caiaphas, who was high priest that year. ¹⁴It was Caiaphas who had counseled the Jews that it was better that one man should die rather than the people.

The description of the Jewish trial is considerably shorter in John. Mark and Matthew speak of a night trial before the high priest and the Sanhedrin as well as a morning session before handing Jesus over to Pilate. The only Jewish legal action described by John is the hearing before Annas. This does not seem to be a formal trial, but rather an interrogation to see if Jesus admits anything revolutionary.

Annas, though no longer high priest himself, must have been a person of substantial influence in Jerusalem. As the patriarch of a family of high priests, he was succeeded by five sons and finally by his son-in-law, Caiaphas. Caiaphas held office from 18 to 36 A.D. John had earlier described Caiaphas' desire to have Jesus put to death because Caiaphas feared for the security of the people (11:50). Yet ironically his plan would unite the dispersed children of God into a new people (11:51-52).

John 18:15-18

Peter's First Denial. ¹⁵Simon Peter and another disciple followed Jesus. Now the other disciple was known to the high priest, and he entered the courtyard of the high priest with Jesus. ¹⁶But Peter stood at the gate outside. So the other disciple, the acquaintance of the high priest, went out and spoke to the gatekeeper and brought Peter in. ¹⁷Then the maid who was the gatekeeper said to Peter, "You are not one of this man's disciples, are you?" He said, "I am not." ¹⁸Now the slaves and the guards were standing around a charcoal fire that they had made, because it was cold, and were warming themselves. Peter was also standing there keeping warm.

Peter's denial of Jesus is woven together with the interrogation before Annas. When Jesus is questioned, he courageously defends his mission; when Peter is questioned, he cowardly denies his association with Jesus. John shifts from one scene to another as the drama develops.

John is the only Gospel writer to introduce "another disciple" into the account of Peter's denial. This unnamed disciple is referred to several times throughout John's narrative and is also called "the other disciple" and "the one whom Jesus loved." This other disciple seems to have been particularly important for the community of John and is shown as a model disciple in the Gospel. He appears in critical scenes in the passion and resurrection accounts: the Last Supper (13:23-26), the denial of Peter, the crucifixion (19:26-27), the empty tomb (20:2-8), and the resurrection appearances (21:7, 20-23). In each scene he is shown in contrast to Peter and seems to come off more favorably.

John 18:19-24

The Inquiry before Annas. [19]The high priest questioned Jesus about his disciples and about his doctrine. [20]Jesus answered him, "I have spoken publicly to the world. I have always taught in a synagogue or in the temple area where all the Jews gather, and in secret I have said nothing. [21]Why ask me? Ask those who heard me what I said to them. They know what I said." [22]When he had said this, one of the temple guards standing there struck Jesus and said, "Is this the way you answer the high priest?" [23]Jesus answered him, "If I have spoken wrongly, testify to the wrong; but if I have spoken rightly, why do you strike me?" [24]Then Annas sent him bound to Caiaphas the high priest.

John calls Annas "high priest" because former high priests continued to be called by this title. As Annas questions him, Jesus responds with open courage as he had throughout his public life. He had spoken openly "to the world." Now his word can be learned from those who heard and followed him. Annas is reduced to silence as Jesus becomes the accuser and Annas the accused.

John minimizes the Jewish mockery reported in the other Gospels. While the synoptic Gospels contain a scene of mockery showing Jesus as the Suffering Servant, John reports only one slap by a temple guard. John will elaborate the Roman mockery as part of his attempt to expand the Roman complicity in the passion.

John 18:25-27

Peter Denies Jesus Again. [25]Now Simon Peter was standing there keeping warm. And they said to him, "You are not one of his disciples, are you?" He denied it and said, "I am not." [26]One of the slaves of the high priest, a relative of the one whose ear Peter had cut off, said, "Didn't I see you in the garden with him?" [27]Again Peter denied it. And immediately the cock crowed.

While Jesus is being sent to Caiaphas, the scene shifts back to the courtyard and is related to Peter's first denial by the warmth of the charcoal fire.

The frequent use of the word "disciple" (vs. 15, 16, 17, 25) emphasizes that Peter's denial was a failure in his discipleship. His courageous enthusiasm at the Last Supper (13:37) is strongly contrasted with his

103

cowardly denial. While the other Gospels mention Peter's tears of repentance, John will expand his account of Peter's reconciliation after the resurrection.

John 18:28-32

The Trial before Pilate. [28]Then they brought Jesus from Caiaphas to the praetorium. It was morning. And they themselves did not enter the praetorium, in order not to be defiled so that they could eat the Passover. [29]So Pilate came out to them and said, "What charge do you bring [against] this man?" [30]They answered and said to him, "If he were not a criminal, we would not have handed him over to you." [31]At this, Pilate said to them, "Take him yourselves, and judge him according to your law." The Jews answered him, "We do not have the right to execute anyone," [32]in order that the word of Jesus might be fulfilled that he said indicating the kind of death he would die.

The trial before Pilate stands at the heart of John's passion narrative. Having reduced the Jewish legal proceedings to a single question asked by Annas, John focuses entirely on the Roman trial. He radically reshapes the historical material from the other Gospels and his own sources in order to heighten the scene dramatically and to center on the theological motifs of his Gospel.

John shifts the scene back and forth from outside the praetorium where the Jews are gathered to the inside where Jesus is held. Pilate moves from the frenzy of the outside to the eloquent defense of Jesus within. This dramatic technique expresses the struggle taking place within Pilate as he weighs his own conviction of Jesus' innocence against the pressure from without to condemn him.

Each scene of the trial is filled with irony; each scene expresses two levels of meaning, evident to the reader but not to the characters within the scene. The emphasis throughout is on the kingship of Jesus. Jesus' condemnation under the pretext that he claimed to be king is the means John uses to reveal the true kingship of Jesus. The true meaning of each scene is often just the reverse of the meaning at first sight.

The introductory verse describes the setting and makes careful note of the time. It is the morning of the day before Passover. The Passover meal would be eaten that evening. Thus we know that John does not present the Last Supper as a Passover meal.

The first scene takes place outside the praetorium. Fear of ritual impurity prevents the Jews from entering the house of a Gentile. They avoid ritual impurity so that they can eat the Passover lamb. Yet ironically they are putting to death the true Passover lamb, the Lamb of God (1:29).

Only John's Gospel gives the reason for the trial before Pilate: the Romans alone had the right to put anyone to death. Pilate wanted the Jews to judge Jesus by their own laws and deal with him accordingly. Yet the Jews protested because the Sanhedrin did not have the authority to crucify anyone. John sees this as a fulfillment of God's plan that Jesus be "lifted up" on the cross (12:32-33).

John 18:33-38a

[33]So Pilate went back into the praetorium and summoned Jesus and said to him, "Are you the King of the Jews?" [34]Jesus answered, "Do you say this on your own or have others told you about me?" [35]Pilate answered, "I am not a Jew, am I? Your own nation and the chief priests handed you over to me. What have you done?" [36]Jesus answered, "My kingdom does not belong to this world. If my kingdom did belong to this world, my attendants [would] be fighting to keep me from being handed over to the Jews. But as it is, my kingdom is not here." [37]So Pilate said to him, "Then you are a king?" Jesus answered, "You say I am a king. For this I was born and for this I came into the world, to testify to the truth. Everyone who belongs to the truth listens to my voice." [38]Pilate said to him, "What is truth?"

The scene moves to the inside of the praetorium for the confrontation between Jesus and Pilate. The first question Pilate asks is the same in all the Gospels: "Are you the king of the Jews?" This is a strong indication that the official accusation made against Jesus by the high priests was subversion against Rome by claiming to be king.

In the other Gospels Jesus replies to Pilate's question with the ambiguous, "You have said so." Yet here Jesus assumes control of the dialogue and gives a careful explanation of his kingship. Jesus is indeed a king, but his kingship is of a very different type. His kingdom is not a political reign belonging to this world, but rather it comes from above.

The mission of Jesus is to reveal the truth. The trial is no longer about Jesus' innocence or guilt, but rather whether or not Pilate will respond to the truth. It is now Pilate who is on trial. Jesus is the truth in that he is the revelation of God in his person, words, and actions. Pilate's question, "What is truth?" shows that he will not recognize the truth made known in Jesus.

John 18:38b-40

When he had said this, he again went out to the Jews and said to them, "I find no guilt in him. ³⁹But you have a custom that I release one prisoner to you at Passover. Do you want me to release to you the King of the Jews?" ⁴⁰They cried out again, "Not this one but Barabbas!" Now Barabbas was a revolutionary.

Going outside again to the crowd, Pilate reveals his verdict: "I find no guilt in him." Yet, even though Pilate knows Jesus is innocent, he yields more and more to those who reject Jesus because he has rejected the truth. Hoping that the crowd will relieve him of the decision he is unwilling to make, Pilate presents to them the ironic choice between Jesus, the true king, and Barabbas, a political insurrectionist. By noting that Barabbas was a revolutionary (the word also means "robber"), John recalls the contrast between the good shepherd whose sheep hear his voice (18:37) and the robber who enters the sheepfold deceptively (10:1-10). The crowds choose the false leader and reject the true messiah who embodies all their hopes.

John 19:1-3

¹Then Pilate took Jesus and had him scourged. ²And the soldiers wove a crown out of thorns and placed it on his head, and clothed him in a purple cloak, ³and they came to him and said, "Hail, King of the Jews!" And they struck him repeatedly.

The scene of Jesus' scourging and mockery forms the structural center of the trial before Pilate. It is preceded by three scenes and is followed by three scenes, each alternating from outside to inside. With dramatic irony, the central theme of the trial, the kingship of Jesus, is displayed.

In Mark and Matthew, the scourging and mocking took place at the end of the trial and were part of Jesus' punishment. In Luke, the mockery was the work of Herod and showed his contempt for Jesus. In John, the scourging and mockery seem to be an attempt by Pilate to placate the crowd and prevent Jesus' crucifixion. In the crowd scenes immediately before and after this one, Pilate proclaims the innocence of Jesus and seeks his release.

Omitting some of the humiliating brutality recorded by Mark and Matthew, John concentrates on those elements of the mockery which imitate kingship: the crown of thorns, the purple cloak, and the acclamations of royalty. The kingship of Jesus is ironically proclaimed as the words of these soldiers foretell the future acclamation of Jesus as king by the Gentiles.

John 19:4-7

> [4]Once more Pilate went out and said to them, "Look, I am bringing him out to you, so that you may know that I find no guilt in him." [5]So Jesus came out, wearing the crown of thorns and the purple cloak. And he said to them, "Behold, the man!" [6]When the chief priests and the guards saw him they cried out, "Crucify him, crucify him!" Pilate said to them, "Take him yourselves and crucify him. I find no guilt in him." [7]The Jews answered, "We have a law, and according to that law he ought to die, because he made himself the Son of God."

Again Pilate appears to the crowd, but this time he has Jesus with him. The theme of kingship is continued as Jesus, wearing his crown and royal cloak, is solemnly presented to his people for acclamation. Pilate's proclamation, "Behold the man," is rich with multi-layered meaning. Pilate is displaying Jesus as an unfortunate and broken man who should not be taken seriously. Yet we also know that Jesus is the suffering Son of Man on his way to glory (12:23).

The Jews hail their king with the shout, "Crucify him!" The verb "cried out" recalls that the same crowd had cried out, "Hosanna . . . the king of Israel," just a few days earlier. Pilate has failed in his attempt to placate the crowd by punishing him and presenting him to the crowd as a harmless pretender.

When Pilate hands the responsibility for dealing with Jesus to the Jews, the real reason for their antagonism becomes clear. They accuse Jesus of blasphemy in claiming himself Son of God; therefore, he ought to die.

John 19:8-11

> [8]Now when Pilate heard this statement, he became even more afraid, [9]and went back into the praetorium and said to Jesus, "Where are you from?" Jesus did not answer him. [10]So Pilate said to him, "Do you not speak to me? Do you not know that I have power to release you and I have power to crucify you?" [11]Jesus answered [him], "You would have no power over me if it had not been given to you from above. For this reason the one who handed me over to you has the greater sin."

This passage parallels the dialogue between Jesus and Pilate in 18:33-38. Both scenes are preceded and followed by the crowd scenes outside. In each, Jesus responds to Pilate in solemn style and becomes his judge. Pilate's questions are on a worldly level, and Jesus' responses indicate that he is on a level above the world.

Pilate's question, "Where are you from?" may have originally been another attempt to rescue Jesus and to lessen his own responsibility. In Luke, Pilate sent Jesus to Herod after hearing that he was from Galilee. However, John uses this question to refer to Jesus' divine origins. Pilate realizes that he is no longer addressing Jesus on the political level, but is responding to the religious claim that Jesus is God's Son.

The heart of the scene is Jesus' statement on power. After Pilate threatens Jesus with his own worldly power to release or crucify him, Jesus speaks on another level. Pilate only has power over Jesus because the Father has given it to him so that Jesus may be glorified. No one takes Jesus' life from him, but he lays it down on his own. As he said, "I have power to lay it down, and power to take it up again" (10:18).

John 19:12-16a

> [12]Consequently, Pilate tried to release him; but the Jews cried out, "If you release him, you are not a Friend of Caesar. Everyone who makes himself a king opposes Caesar."
> [13]When Pilate heard these words he brought Jesus out and seated him on the judge's bench in the place called Stone Pavement, in Hebrew, Gabbatha. [14]It was preparation day for Passover, and it was about noon. And he said to the Jews, "Behold, your king!" [15]They cried out, "Take him away, take him away! Crucify him!" Pilate said to them, "Shall I crucify your king?" The chief priests answered, "We have no king but Caesar." [16]Then he handed him over to them to be crucified.

John shows clearly Pilate's real reason for yielding to the Jewish demands. The crowds used political blackmail against him by threatening to denounce him to Rome. It is suggested that Pilate bore the honorific title, "Friend of Caesar," bestowed on meritorious officials. If Pilate is accused of benevolence toward a rival of the emperor he will be harshly punished for disloyalty.

Pilate again brings Jesus out of the praetorium and seats him on the judge's bench before the crowd. This gesture captures the irony of the entire trial. Though it seems that Jesus is on trial, the real judge throughout is Jesus himself. His questions place Pilate on trial and by condemning Jesus, those who reject Jesus are really judging themselves.

All four Gospels set the day of Jesus' death on a Friday, the day before the Sabbath. Yet John differs from the others in stating this day's relationship to the Passover. The synoptic Gospels show that Jesus died on the first day of Passover, while John states that it was Preparation Day, the day before the feast began. Though the historical reality is uncertain, each Gospel associates Jesus' death with aspects of the Passover feast.

In John, Jesus is handed over to be crucified at the very hour the Passover lambs begin to be ritually slaughtered in the temple. While thousands of lambs are being killed in preparation for the great feast of Jewish liberation, the Lamb of God who takes away the sin of the world (1:29) is offered up on the cross.

The final words of the chief priests, "We have no king but Caesar," proclaim a dreadful judgment upon themselves. Israel had always claimed God alone as its true king. This kingship was made visible in the anointed king of the House of David and it was expected that the future Messiah would come to establish God's reign on earth. Now the Jews are rejecting their messianic king and, with dreadful blasphemy, give their allegiance to Tiberius, the deranged emperor exiled to Capri.

John 19:16b-22

The Crucifixion of Jesus. So they took Jesus, [17]and carrying the cross himself he went out to what is called the Place of the Skull, in Hebrew, Golgotha. [18]There they crucified him, and with him two others, one on either side, with Jesus in the middle. [19]Pilate also had an inscription written and put on the cross. It read, "Jesus the Nazorean, the King of the Jews." [20]Now many of the Jews read this inscription, because the place where Jesus was crucified was near the city; and it was written in Hebrew, Latin, and Greek. [21]So the chief priests of the Jews said to Pilate, "Do not write 'The King of the Jews,' but that he said, 'I am the King of the Jews.' " [22]Pilate answered, "What I have written, I have written."

John notes that as Jesus is taken out for crucifixion, he alone carries the cross. The synoptic Gospels make Simon of Cyrene an image of discipleship as he carries the cross, but John emphasizes Jesus' control of his own destiny. Here John continues to show that no one takes Jesus' life from him, but that he lays it down on his own (10:18). Also, John wants to allude to the Old Testament figure of Isaac, the sacrificial victim who carried the wood for the offering of himself.

The theme of kingship, so central to the trial scenes, continues in the crucifixion account. As the crucified king, Jesus is placed in the middle of the two criminals, the position of honor. The inscription over the cross proclaims Jesus' kingship in the three pertinent languages of the empire: Hebrew, Latin, and Greek. John is stressing the universal kingship of Jesus, proclaimed from the cross to the whole world. Despite the objections of the chief priests, Pilate insists on leaving the inscription stand as written, a final ironic proclamation from the defiant procurator.

John 19:23-24

[23]When the soldiers had crucified Jesus, they took his clothes and divided them into four shares, a share for each soldier. They also took his tunic, but the tunic was seamless, woven in one piece from the top down. [24]So they said to one another, "Let's not tear it, but cast lots for it to see whose it will be," in order that the passage of scripture might be fulfilled [that says]:

"They divided my garments among them,
and for my vesture they cast lots."

This is what the soldiers did.

While the other Gospel writers speak of casting lots to divide Jesus' garments, John amplifies the scene with several additions. He distinguishes between the outer garments of Jesus that were divided into four shares, and the inner tunic which was not divided. Though the other evangelists refer to Psalm 22:19, John explicitly cites the verse and shows the two parallel lines referring to different items of apparel.

The seamless tunic is clearly the focus of symbolism for John. The high priest's tunic is described similarly in other writings, thus John may be showing that Jesus died, not only as a king, but also as a priest. The priesthood of Jesus is certainly a New Testament idea and is particularly developed in the Letter to the Hebrews.

The undivided garment also symbolizes the unity of Jesus and the Church. While his other garments were divided into four parts, representing the four corners of the earth, the future expanse of the Church, the seamless garment represents the unity of that Church. Such unity is the focus of Jesus' final prayer at the Last Supper and is an important theme throughout the Gospel (10:16; 11:52; 17:11, 21-23).

John 19:25-27

²⁵Standing by the cross of Jesus were his mother and his mother's sister, Mary the wife of Clopas, and Mary of Magdala. ²⁶When Jesus saw his mother and the disciple there whom he loved, he said to his mother, "Woman, behold, your son." ²⁷Then he said to the disciple, "Behold, your mother." And from that hour the disciple took her into his home.

The women at the cross of Jesus are described differently in John's Gospel. The other evangelists place the women at a distance looking on. John intensifies the drama by placing them at the foot of the cross and by adding the mother of Jesus and the beloved disciple to the scene.

The scene with Jesus' mother and the beloved disciple has many levels of meaning which is typical of John's writing. On a purely natural plane it shows Jesus' care for his mother. He entrusts her to the charge of his beloved disciple before his own death. Yet there are many indications that John had something more profound in mind than simply filial care. Though both figures are clearly historical persons, John never gives us their personal names. It seems that their importance for the Gospel lies in their symbolic and spiritual roles.

The wedding at Cana (2:1-12), the only other scene in which John speaks of Jesus' mother, has several similarities to this one. In both instances she is addressed as "Woman," an unusual title when speaking to one's own mother. In both scenes "the hour" of Jesus becomes central; at Cana his hour had not yet come, and here his hour of glorification is upon him. We also see Jesus, within the context of his approaching death, speak about a woman giving birth (16:21). Here too he uses the words "woman" and "hour" and speaks about his glorification in terms of the pains and joys of childbirth. Thus, the maternal role of Mary belongs not primarily to the physical life of Jesus, but to the "hour" of Jesus when the Christian community is born.

At the foot of the cross Jesus leaves behind the new community of his disciples. This is consistent with the view of the other Gospels in which Jesus indicates that his mother and brothers and sisters are his disciples, those who do the will of the Father (Mark 3:31-35; Matt 12:46-50; Luke 8:19-21). In John, the mother of Jesus becomes the mother of the disciples as the new spiritual family is formed by the spirit of Jesus released at his death.

There are many Old Testament passages in which Israel is symbolized by a woman giving birth to a new people (for example, Isa 54:1; 66:7-9). The woman in Revelation 12:1-18, in a similar image, gives birth to the messiah. After her child was "caught up to God and his throne," the woman continued life on earth with "the rest of her offspring," the Christian disciples, "those who keep God's commandments and bear witness to Jesus." Thus, as the beloved disciple in John's Gospel represents ideal discipleship, so the mother of Jesus is an image of the Church, caring for and placed in the care of Jesus' disciples, who become her children and Jesus' brothers and sisters.

John may also be referring to the woman of Genesis 3:15 and the enmity between her offspring and that of the Satan/serpent. John shows several parallels to the creation accounts: he begins his Gospel with the same three words used to begin the Book of Genesis, and notes that the place of Jesus' suffering, death, and resurrection was a "garden" (18:1; 19:41).

Jesus speaks of the offspring of Satan (8:44) and says that his own "hour" is the hour of Satan's fall (12:23, 31). The mother of Jesus, the "woman," is the new Eve whose offspring form the new people of God.

John 19:28-30

>²⁸After this, aware that everything was now finished, in order that the scripture might be fulfilled, Jesus said, "I thirst." ²⁹There was a vessel filled with common wine. So they put a sponge soaked in wine on a sprig of hyssop and put it up to his mouth. ³⁰When Jesus had taken the wine, he said, "It is finished." And bowing his head, he handed over the spirit.

Having symbolized the birth of the Christian community at the foot of the cross, John tells us that Jesus realized everything was finished. He could now bring to completion what the Scriptures had foretold about the necessity of a suffering messiah. His death would fulfill his life's mission, the accomplishment of his Father's will.

Jesus' words from the cross, "I thirst," express his desire to fulfill his Father's will. He is to "drink the cup" which the Father gave him to drink. Jesus' drinking of the wine literally fulfills Psalm 69:22, "In my thirst they gave me vinegar to drink." Only after Jesus drinks the cup of suffering and death can he become the source of living water for all who thirst (7:37-38). Only after Jesus gives the Spirit in his glorification "rivers of living water" will flow within those who believe in him (7:39).

John alone mentions the hyssop plant used to give Jesus the wine. It was hyssop that was used to sprinkle the saving blood of the Passover lamb in Exodus 12:22. John evokes the Old Testament symbolism to show that the blood of Jesus establishes the new covenant. Crucified at the time the paschal lambs were being slaughtered in the temple, the dying Jesus is shown to be the "Lamb of God who takes away the sin of the world" (1:29).

Jesus' last words, "It is finished," are very different from the agonizing cries of Jesus in Mark and Matthew. These words symbolize the triumphant completion as Jesus accepts his death as the fulfillment of the Father's plan. As he dies, Jesus hands over the spirit and begins the new life of the Christian community.

John 19:31-37

The Blood and Water. ³¹Now since it was preparation day, in order that the bodies might not remain on the cross on the sabbath, for the sabbath day of that week was a solemn one, the Jews asked Pilate that their legs be broken and they be taken down. ³²So the soldiers came and broke the legs of the first and then of the other one who was crucified with Jesus. ³³But when they came to Jesus and saw that he was already dead, they did not break his legs, ³⁴but one soldier thrust his lance into his side, and immediately blood and water flowed out. ³⁵An eyewitness has testified, and his testimony is true; he knows that he is speaking the truth, so that you also may [come to] believe. ³⁶For this happened so that the scripture passage might be fulfilled:

113

"Not a bone of it will be broken."
³⁷And again another passage says:
"They will look upon him whom they have pierced."

In each of the Gospels the death of Jesus is followed by miraculous signs that express the meaning of his death. The synoptic Gospels surround the scene of the cross with extraordinary incidents, such as the tearing of the temple veil, the earthquake and opening of the tombs, and the confession of faith by the centurion. In John, however, the signs which express the meaning and results of his death are localized in the body of Jesus.

On a historical level, John carefully notes that the legs of the other two bodies were broken while Jesus' legs were not. The legs were broken to hasten their death because the Sabbath was drawing near and the bodies were to be taken down from the crosses. However, since Jesus was already dead, they did not break his legs. John's interest here is clearly on a deeper level and it is related to the Passover about to begin. The Scripture passages quoted are from Exodus 12:46 which commands that none of the bones of the paschal lamb be broken, and from Psalm 34:20 which assures the same protection from mutilation for the just man. Again Jesus is shown as the sacrificial Lamb who fulfills the ancient Passover and brings to salvation all who follow him.

John states that when the side of Jesus is pierced with a lance, immediately blood and water flow out. There are many medical theories that explain how this unusual phenomenon could happen. We may begin by assuming John is describing something that really happened, whether naturally or miraculously. His appeal to the eyewitness testimony confirms this assumption. Yet, clearly John has a deeper and more theological reason for emphasizing this event. The thrust of the lance demonstrates for the witnesses that Jesus was truly dead. John shows from his death there flows new life for all who follow him.

In John 7:38-39 Jesus refers to a Scripture passage: "Rivers of living water will flow from within him." John explains that Jesus is here referring to the Spirit that believers were to receive when Jesus had been glorified. Thus the flowing water from within Jesus symbolizes the life-giving Spirit given to the Church through the death and resurrection of Jesus.

To understand the union of blood with the water, we refer to a related passage from the same school of writing, 1 John 5:6-8. Here it states that Jesus "came through water and blood, not by water alone."

It also says that there are three that testify, "the Spirit, the water, and the blood." And the testimony is this: "God gave us eternal life, and this life is in his Son" (1 John 5:11). The Spirit was not able to come until Jesus had departed (John 16:7), until he had shed his blood. Now the life-giving effects of both the water and the blood are able to touch all who believe.

The only other reference to the blood of Jesus is in John 6:53-56. In speaking about the Eucharist, Jesus says that whoever drinks his blood has eternal life. Thus the blood and water symbolize the Eucharist and baptism, the two principal means by which the followers of Jesus share in his life through the Spirit. Therefore, at the moment of his death Jesus forms his Church, delivers forth his Spirit upon it, and pours forth the means to share in his eternal life.

John 19:38-42

The Burial of Jesus. [38]After this, Joseph of Arimathea, secretly a disciple of Jesus for fear of the Jews, asked Pilate if he could remove the body of Jesus. And Pilate permitted it. So he came and took his body. [39]Nicodemus, the one who had first come to him at night, also came bringing a mixture of myrrh and aloes weighing about one hundred pounds. [40]They took the body of Jesus and bound it with burial cloths along with the spices, according to the Jewish burial custom. [41]Now in the place where he had been crucified there was a garden, and in the garden a new tomb, in which no one had yet been buried. [42]So they laid Jesus there because of the Jewish preparation day; for the tomb was close by.

Like in the other Gospels, Joseph of Arimathea asks Pilate for the body of Jesus. Receiving Pilate's permission, Joseph lays Jesus in a tomb because the Sabbath is quickly approaching. John, however, adds his own details to this concluding scene of the passion.

John describes Joseph and Nicodemus as a different type of believer. They were both Jews who believed in Jesus but did not yet have the courage to profess their faith openly. Joseph was "secretly a disciple of Jesus for fear of the Jews." Nicodemus, mentioned only in John's Gospel, secretly approached Jesus at night (3:1-21). John points to the example of Joseph and Nicodemus to show that once Jesus has been lifted up, he will draw everyone to himself (12:32).

The other evangelists describe Jesus' burial as a preparation for the resurrection; they include in their accounts the closing of the tomb with a stone, and the women carefully observing the location of the tomb so they can return to anoint Jesus after the Sabbath. John, however, describes the burial scene as the conclusion of the passion by continuing the theme of Jesus' kingship. As Jesus was hailed as king during his trial, and publicly proclaimed as king on the cross, so now he is buried as a king. The huge amount of myrrh and aloes and the new tomb are elements of a burial befitting a king.

John 20:1-10

The Empty Tomb. ¹On the first day of the week, Mary of Magdala came to the tomb early in the morning, while it was still dark, and saw the stone removed from the tomb. ²So she ran and went to Simon Peter and to the other disciple whom Jesus loved, and told them, "They have taken the Lord from the tomb, and we don't know where they put him." ³So Peter and the other disciple went out and came to the tomb. ⁴They both ran, but the other disciple ran faster than Peter and arrived at the tomb first; ⁵he bent down and saw the burial cloths there, but did not go in. ⁶When Simon Peter arrived after him, he went into the tomb and saw the burial cloths there, ⁷and the cloth that had covered his head, not with the burial cloths but rolled up in a separate place. ⁸Then the other disciple also went in, the one who had arrived at the tomb first, and he saw and believed. ⁹For they did not yet understand the scripture that he had to rise from the dead. ¹⁰Then the disciples returned home.

Each Gospel writer begins the resurrection narrative by noting the day and the time. They are consistent in referring to early Sunday morning, the first day of the week. Yet, while the synoptic Gospels describe the hour as dawn, John notes that it was still dark. This fits well with his symbolic contrast of light and darkness throughout the Gospel. It was still dark because the light of Jesus' presence was gone for the disciples since they had not yet experienced the light of faith in the resurrection.

John identifies only Mary Magdalene at the tomb, though the "we" in verse 2 hints at an earlier tradition that there were other women with her. Unlike in the other Gospels, John does not specify why Mary Magdalene came to the tomb. While the other writers describe an angelic message, it seems from this narrative Mary concluded that Jesus' body was absent when she saw the tomb no longer sealed by the stone. Thinking that the body must have been stolen, she ran to tell Peter and the other disciple.

The unnamed disciple, here called "the other disciple whom Jesus loved," is introduced in the resurrection accounts of this Gospel. He is depicted again with Peter and is shown to be a model disciple. He has the edge on Peter in both speed and insight. The purpose of the contrast is not to detract from Peter, but to show that the other disciple is a model for all disciples because he is closely bonded to Jesus in love. Though arriving first at the tomb, the other disciple does not go in, but defers to Peter. By noting Peter's entry into the tomb first, this evangelist shows he is familiar with the dominant resurrection tradition that recognizes Peter as the chief witness of the resurrection.

The whole scene builds up to the climactic verse, "He saw and believed." The beloved disciple was led to belief by seeing Jesus' burial cloths lying where his body had been. If the grave had been robbed, certainly the wrappings would have been taken with the body. The scene is a strong contrast to the one depicting the emergence of Lazarus from the tomb, in which John gives a detailed account of the various wrappings that still bound the risen body.

John 20:11-18

The Appearance to Mary of Magdala. [11]But Mary stayed outside the tomb weeping. And as she wept, she bent over into the tomb [12]and saw two angels in white sitting there, one at the head and one at the feet where the body of Jesus had been. [13]And they said to her, "Woman, why are you weeping?" She said to them, "They have taken my Lord, and I don't know where they laid him." [14]When she had said this, she turned around and saw Jesus there, but did not know it was Jesus. [15]Jesus said to her, "Woman, why are you weeping? Whom are you looking for?" She thought it was the gardener and said to him, "Sir, if you carried him away, tell me where you laid him, and I will take him." [16]Jesus said to her, "Mary!" She turned and said to him in Hebrew, "Rabbouni," which means Teacher. [17]Jesus said to her, "Stop holding on to me, for I have not yet ascended to the Father. But go to my brothers and tell them, 'I am going to my Father and your Father, to my God and your God.' " [18]Mary of Magdala went and announced to the disciples, "I have seen the Lord," and what he told her.

The account of Jesus' appearance to Mary Magdalene was originally a separate tradition from the discovery of the empty tomb in verses 1-10. The empty tomb emphasizes the reality that the risen Jesus is a bodily presence and is continuous with his earthly existence. The appearance narrative focuses on his transformation and the difficulty in recognizing his presence. John links the two accounts with the transition in verse 11.

The attention given to the difficulty in recognizing the risen Jesus is a defense of the reality of the appearances. If the followers of Jesus had been expecting and anticipating his appearance, their experience could be attributed to a psychological impression. Their difficulty in recognizing Jesus also demonstrates that the reality of Jesus has changed; his followers now experience him in a new way.

Jesus asks Mary Magdalene, "Whom are you looking for?" Mary's search for Jesus represents the search of all followers of Jesus. The scene is charged with intimacy and affection for him. Only when she hears his voice, when Jesus calls her by name, does she recognize him. John is telling his readers that in the spoken word of Jesus they have the means of recognizing his presence. Just as the sheep recognize the voice of the shepherd when he calls their name (10:3-4), Jesus calls his followers personally to a relationship with him.

Luke's accounts of the ascension express the termination of Jesus' resurrection appearances. John's understanding is very different. Ascension in John's Gospel is not separated from the resurrection. Jesus continually describes the goal of his life in terms of being lifted up and going to the Father. On the cross Jesus has already entered into the process of glorification. Resurrection from the dead involves ascension to God's presence and exaltation at God's right hand. Jesus is lifted up on the cross; he is raised up from the dead; and he ascends to the Father. All is part of his "hour," his exaltation and glorification.

Considering this understanding of Jesus' ascension, we can better understand his words to Mary, "Stop holding on to me, for I have not yet ascended to the Father." She is trying to hold on to Jesus in the same way she had clung to him during his earthly ministry. Jesus indicates that his permanent presence will come only with the gift of the Spirit as he ascends to the Father. In speaking of his ascension in the discourse on the bread of life, Jesus said, "It is the spirit that gives life, while the flesh is of no avail" (6:63). Mary must not cling to Jesus as if he were still in the flesh; rather she is commanded to go and prepare the disciples for that coming of Jesus when the Spirit will be given.

The Spirit will create a renewed, life-giving relationship, not only with Jesus but also with the Father. Jesus describes his ascension as his "going to my Father and your Father, to my God and your God." Jesus' filial relationship to the Father is now to be shared with his disciples. The words of John's prologue are fulfilled, "To those who did accept him he gave power to become children of God" (1:12). The giving of the Spirit will beget the believing disciples as children of the Father.

John 20:19-23

Appearance to the Disciples. ¹⁹On the evening of that first day of the week, when the doors were locked, where the disciples were, for fear of the Jews, Jesus came and stood in their midst and said to them, "Peace be with you." ²⁰When he had said this, he showed them his hands and his side. The disciples rejoiced when they saw the Lord. ²¹[Jesus] said to them again, "Peace be with you. As the Father has sent me, so I send you." ²²And when he had said this, he breathed on them and said to them, "Receive the holy Spirit. ²³Whose sins you forgive are forgiven them, and whose sins you retain are retained."

In describing the appearance of the risen Jesus, John shows that Jesus is transformed and is no longer bound by material conditions such as locked doors. Yet the risen body is also corporeal, evidenced by the wounds in his hands and side. Even more significantly, the concentration on Jesus' wounds establishes the continuity between the crucifixion and the resurrection. Jesus who was lifted up on the cross is the same Jesus who now stands before his disciples.

John focuses on the presence of the risen Jesus and on what his presence means and brings to the disciples. Here Jesus fulfills many of his promises given in the Last Discourse, especially the peace and joy which his presence brings. At the Last Supper, after promising to send the Spirit, Jesus left his disciples with the gift of peace. In urging them not to fear he associated his gift of peace to his promise to return to them (14:27-28). Now that he has returned to them, he grants his peace which is his enduring and saving presence given through the Spirit.

Also in the Last Discourse Jesus assures the disciples they will rejoice when he returns to them. "You are now in anguish; but I will see you again, and your hearts will rejoice, and no one will take your joy away from you" (16:22). This lasting and unworldly sense of peace and joy was characteristic of the end time anticipated in the Old Testament. John shows that this period is fulfilled as Jesus returns to give forth his Spirit.

In communicating the Spirit to the disciples, Jesus commissions them to continue the salvific mission he received from the Father. Through the power of the Spirit Jesus will be present to the disciples on their mission, just as the Father was present with Jesus on his mission (13:20). Now the disciples will show forth Jesus, as the Spirit of truth testifies to him (15:26), and as the Spirit teaches them everything and reminds them of all that Jesus told them (16:26).

As Jesus delivers forth the Holy Spirit to his disciples, he breathes on them. As God blew spirit or breath of life into humanity at creation (Gen 2:7), Jesus breathes his Spirit as God's people are re-created. In another image the dry bones of Ezekiel's vision are brought to life when the spirit is breathed into them (Ezek 37). So, too, the Spirit gives eternal life to those who follow Jesus in the new creation.

The mission of the disciples is described as the forgiveness of sins and the retaining of sins. They will continue to participate in the work of the "Lamb of God who takes away the sin of the world" (1:29). Jesus came into the world to save it, yet some are condemned because they do not believe in him (3:17-18). Like Jesus, the disciples cause people to judge themselves; some come into the light and receive forgiveness of sins, others remain in darkness. Jesus gives his disciples a power over sin that is to be exercised through the Holy Spirit as they are sent to continue his work.

John 20:24-29

> **Thomas.** [24]Thomas, called Didymus, one of the Twelve, was not with them when Jesus came. [25]So the other disciples said to him, "We have seen the Lord." But he said to them, "Unless I see the mark of the nails in his hands and put my finger into the nailmarks and put my hand into his side, I will not believe." [26]Now a week later his disciples were again inside and Thomas was with them. Jesus came, although the doors were locked, and stood in their midst and said, "Peace be with you." [27]Then he said to Thomas, "Put your finger here and see my hands, and bring your hand and put it into my side, and do not be unbelieving, but believe." [28]Thomas answered and said to him, "My Lord and my God!" [29]Jesus said to him, "Have you come to believe because you have seen me? Blessed are those who have not seen and have believed."

Only in John's Gospel does Thomas play a significant role. He speaks at the death of Lazarus (11:16) and at the Last Supper (14:5). In each situation his misunderstanding serves to bring out the truth in Jesus' words. In this resurrection scene Thomas' skepticism leads to an indisputable confirmation of the reality of Jesus' risen presence.

The other disciples have already seen the risen Lord and have believed in him, but Thomas does not accept their word. Instead he seeks visible and tangible proof of the resurrection. His attitude is the same as those reprimanded by Jesus when he said, "Unless you people see signs and wonders, you will not believe" (4:48). To all such followers Jesus says, "Do not be unbelieving, but believe." When Jesus sarcastically offers Thomas the tangible proof he demands, Thomas becomes a believer.

Thomas' skepticism develops into the supreme profession of Christian faith: "My Lord and my God!" Jesus is given many titles in John's Gospel: Word of God, Rabbi, Messiah, Prophet, King of Israel, Son of God, and others. Yet nothing more profound could be said of him than Thomas' climactic exclamation. Thomas addresses Jesus in the same way that Israel addressed Yahweh.

Up to this point, belief in Jesus has come through the experience of seeing him. Yet, now the Gospel writer speaks about followers of Jesus who will believe without having seen him. The final words of Jesus contrast two different but equally valid forms of belief: the belief that comes from seeing him and the belief that comes through the word of his disciples. Through the invisible presence of Jesus by means of the Spirit, a new type of faith is possible. It is this kind of belief that will allow all people to come to know the blessings experienced in the Risen Lord.

John 20:30-31

Conclusion. [30]Now Jesus did many other signs in the presence of [his] disciples that are not written in this book. [31]But these are written that you may [come to] believe that Jesus is the Messiah, the Son of God, and that through this belief you may have life in his name.

These verses form a conclusion to all that has been recorded in John's Gospel. The writer states that his book cannot be a complete account of the ministry of Jesus and cannot capture the inexhaustible fullness of what Jesus has done. The "signs" in John's Gospel are the wondrous deeds of Jesus that invite the beholder or the reader to belief. John interprets seven such signs in chapters 1–12. Yet, the appearances of Jesus to his disciples must also be "signs" since they too draw the participant to the choice of belief or disbelief. Those who believe penetrate beyond the marvelous deeds, to an understanding of the truth about Jesus.

John is the only evangelist to conclude with a statement of purpose for his Gospel. It is written so that those who have not seen may share the same belief as those who have seen. The goal of that belief is the understanding that Jesus is the Messiah, the Son of God. It is the same belief that Martha professed at the raising of Lazarus, the last of Jesus' seven signs (11:27). It is only in him that Lazarus came to life. It is only when one comes to believe Jesus is truly sent from God, that he is truly Son of God, that one can receive true life which is a gift of God alone.

John 21:1-14

The Appearance to the Seven Disciples. [1]After this, Jesus revealed himself again to his disciples at the Sea of Tiberias. He revealed himself in this way. [2]Together were Simon Peter, Thomas called Didymus, Nathanael from Cana in Galilee, Zebedee's sons, and two others of his disciples. [3]Simon Peter said to them, "I am going fishing." They said to him, "We also will come with you." So they went out and got into the boat, but that night they caught nothing. [4]When it was already dawn, Jesus was standing on the shore; but the disciples did not realize that it was Jesus. [5]Jesus said to them, "Children, have you caught anything to eat?" They answered him, "No." [6]So he said to them, "Cast the net over the right side of the boat and you will find something." So they cast it, and were not able to pull it in because of the number of fish. [7]So the disciple whom Jesus loved said to Peter, "It is the Lord." When Simon Peter heard that it was the Lord, he tucked in his garment, for he was lightly clad, and jumped into the sea. [8]The other disciples came in the boat, for they were not far from shore, only about a hundred yards, dragging the net with the fish. [9]When they climbed out on shore, they saw a charcoal fire with fish on it and bread. [10]Jesus said to them, "Bring some of the fish you just caught." [11]So Simon Peter went over and dragged the net ashore full of one hundred fifty-three large fish. Even though there were so many, the net was not torn. [12]Jesus said to them, "Come, have breakfast." And none of the disciples dared to ask him, "Who are you?" because they realized it was the Lord. [13]Jesus came over and took the bread and gave it to them, and in like manner the fish. [14]This was now the third time Jesus was revealed to his disciples after being raised from the dead.

The final chapter of John is generally regarded as an addition to the original Gospel which ended with John's powerful assertion that eternal life in God comes only when one believes that Jesus is sent from God and is the Son of God (20:31). There are enough stylistic differences to convince us that the writer of this final chapter was not the writer of the Gospel's core. Yet it is also clear that the writer shared the same general world of Johannine thought and linked this chapter with the previous ones by many theological and literary parallels. It must have been added very early by a disciple of the evangelist since it is present in every ancient manuscript and is clearly a genuine part of the canonical Gospel.

The chapter places more emphasis on the community aspects of Jesus' resurrection and stresses themes pertinent to the life of the Church. The author intended to complete the Gospel by highlighting the apostolic mission of the Church, the eucharistic presence of the Lord, Peter's pastoral authority, and the role of the beloved disciple.

The scene opens at the Sea of Tiberias in Galilee where the author says twice, "Jesus revealed himself." At the beginning of the Gospel, John the Baptist stated the whole purpose of his ministry was that Jesus might be "revealed" to Israel (1:31). Jesus worked his first sign at Cana to "reveal" his glory (2:11). Jesus healed the blind man so that the works of God might be "revealed" through him (9:3). At the Last Supper Jesus prayed to the Father, "I revealed your name to those whom you gave me" (17:6). As Jesus revealed himself through his works and again in his resurrection, he was revealing God. Now the Gospel is completed as Jesus shows forth God's life and love to the community of believers (1 John 1:2; 4:9).

Having returned to Galilee, the disciples resume the occupation they know best. However, their fishing is unsuccessful, for without Jesus they can do nothing (15:5). The futility of their efforts during the night, followed by their tremendous success at dawn when Jesus is present, continues the frequent contrast of light and darkness throughout the Gospel.

Again we see the interrelationship between Peter and the disciple whom Jesus loved. The anonymous disciple is the more perceptive and recognizes Jesus. Yet Peter is shown to have the first place in the apostolic ministry. It is Peter who jumps into the sea, who hands in the catch of fish, and who receives the commission from Jesus.

The great catch of fish symbolically represents the apostolic mission Jesus gives to the community of his disciples (Luke 5:10). The number of fish, one hundred fifty-three, in some way emphasizes the completeness and universality of the mission. St. Jerome speculates there were one hundred fifty-three varieties of fish known at the time. The net that was not torn despite the huge catch suggests the unity of the Church. As the net of fish is drawn ashore at Jesus' invitation to eat, we are reminded of his words, "When I am lifted up from the earth, I will draw everyone to myself" (12:32). The great catch seems to be a symbolic equivalent to the apostolic commission Jesus gives his followers at the end of Matthew: "Go and make disciples of all the nations" (Matt 28:19).

The meal on the shore reminds the reader of the Eucharist and associates it with the risen Christ's presence. The description of Jesus' action with the bread and the fish echoes John's account of the meal eaten after the multiplication of the loaves and fish (6:11). Both scenes take place by the Sea of Tiberias, and the multiplication scene is followed by Jesus' extended discourse on the Eucharist. Here the missionary disciples gather with their great catch to share in the meal of communion prepared by the risen Lord.

John 21:15-19

Jesus and Peter. [15]When they had finished breakfast, Jesus said to Simon Peter, "Simon, son of John, do you love me more than these?" He said to him, "Yes, Lord, you know that I love you." He said to him, "Feed my lambs." [16]He then said to him a second time, "Simon, son of John, do you love me?" He said to him, "Yes, Lord, you know that I love you." He said to him, "Tend my sheep." [17]He said to him the third time, "Simon, son of John, do you love me?" Peter was distressed that he had said to him a third time, "Do you love me?" and he said to him, "Lord, you know everything; you know that I love you." [Jesus] said to him, "Feed my sheep. [18]Amen, amen, I say to you, when you were younger, you used to dress yourself and go where you wanted; but when you grow old, you will stretch out your hands, and someone else will dress you and lead you where you do not want to go." [19]He said this signifying by what kind of death he would glorify God. And when he had said this, he said to him, "Follow me."

Jesus now gives Peter his complete attention. The charcoal fire recalls the fire in the courtyard when Peter had denied Jesus (18:18). The three questions asked of Peter and his responses counteract his earlier denial; here his faithful responses are a symbolic restoration of Peter to discipleship. The devoted love for Jesus expressed by Peter is the essence of true discipleship.

Jesus' threefold command to Peter, "Feed my sheep," establishes him as the shepherd of God's flock. Throughout the Old Testament God is described as the shepherd of Israel (Ezek 34; Ps 23). God delegates authority by divine commission to those chosen to rule over the flock (2 Sam 5:2). John 10 describes Jesus as the good shepherd who leads his flock and extends personal and sacrificial care for them. Here Jesus assigns responsibility for the flock to Peter and commissions him to lead the flock according to his own example. This kind of pastoral care does not accent the shepherd's superior position, but rather his individual care and total dedication to the flock.

In his description of the model shepherd, Jesus says, "A good shepherd lays down his life for the sheep" (10:11). Here it is particularly significant that a description of Peter's death follows the command to tend the sheep. Peter's martyrdom will prove the sincerity of his love, for Jesus said, "No one has greater love than this, to lay down one's life for one's friends" (15:13).

The saying of Jesus in verse 18 was probably a proverb concerning youth and old age. Here it is specifically applied to the death of Peter. With his freedom taken away, Peter will be led to the place of execution where he will stretch out his hands in crucifixion. The death which "glorifies God" is standard Christian terminology for martyrdom. By the time the Gospel was written, the author would have known that Peter died a martyr's death and perhaps even that he had been crucified on Vatican Hill in Rome.

At the Last Supper Peter had urged Jesus to allow him to follow. Jesus responded, "Where I am going, you cannot follow me now, though you will follow me later." Peter argued, "Why can't I follow you now? I will lay down my life for you." Knowing that Peter was incapable of such discipleship, Jesus predicted his three denials (13:36-38). Yet now, having forgiven and empowered Peter, Jesus says to him, "Follow me." Only now is Peter capable of true discipleship as he follows Jesus even to the point of laying down his life for him.

John 21:20-23

The Beloved Disciple. ²⁰Peter turned and saw the disciple following whom Jesus loved, the one who had also reclined upon his chest during the supper and had said, "Master, who is the one who will betray you?" ²¹When Peter saw him, he said to Jesus, "Lord, what about him?" ²²Jesus said to him, "What if I want him to remain until I come? What concern is it of yours? You follow me." ²³So the word spread among the brothers that that disciple would not die. But Jesus had not told him that he would not die, just "What if I want him to remain until I come? [What concern is it of yours?]"

Attention turns to the disciple whom Jesus loved. In response to Peter's question, Jesus points out that the other disciple also has a special destiny. In contrast to Peter's untimely death, the beloved disciple is to remain. His witness, to live out a long life in faithful love, is a form of discipleship just as valid as Peter's.

The author's statement that Jesus had not told the beloved disciple he would not die, was probably occasioned by the death, or the imminent death, of the disciple. The community for whom the Gospel was written must have been deeply disturbed, particularly if they had expected him not to die. The beloved disciple must have been one of the last of the original disciples to die. This dying out of the apostolic generation was a challenge to the faith of many, since it was a belief that Jesus was to have returned first.

John 21:24-25

Conclusion. ²⁴It is this disciple who testifies to these things and has written them, and we know that his testimony is true. ²⁵There are also many other things that Jesus did, but if these were to be described individually, I do not think the whole world would contain the books that would be written.

The final verses of the Gospel make it clear that the importance of the beloved disciple is not in his continued life, but in his witness to the good news. It is his eyewitness testimony that forms the secure foundation of the present Gospel. His testimony is "true" not only because of his personal presence during the ministry of Jesus, but also because it concerns Jesus who is the truth (14:6). It is "testimony" not only because it comes from an eyewitness, but because the Spirit of truth testifies to Jesus (15:26).

The final comment is a literary exaggeration that explains why no attempt has been made to include all the things that Jesus did. No book can even begin to express the meaning of Jesus' life and its infinite fullness for us. The words of John's Gospel could never contain the Word made flesh who is forever the way, the truth, and the life.